Keep it simple and strong

Survival Tourism English

prof. Moon, young soo/ Cheon, jae yun

Keep it simple and strong

Survival Tourism English

prof. Moon, young soo/ Cheon, jae yun

- **Focus on the true tourism English.**
- **Maximize your tourism English.**
- **Practice situations in different contexts.**

BAEKSAN
Publishing Co

Preface

한 때 한류열풍이 뜸하다 싶었는데 2010년을 넘어서면서 그 기세가 여느 때와 같지 않습니다. 역사의 흐름이 우리 대한민국에게 또 한 번의 기회를 주고 있습니다. 좋은 의미에서 우리나라 관광업계는 긴장해야 합니다. 다시 말해서 그 한류 폭풍이 대한민국 관광 현장에서 느끼도록 해야 한다는 것입니다. 그리고 이렇듯이 한국에 관심을 갖는 사람들을 국내로 끌어들이기 위해서 끊임없는 연구와 개발이 요구됩니다.

지금 한국 관광의 미래를 위해서 강의실과 연구실에서 골몰하는 젊은 학생들에게 큰 격려를 보냅니다. 잘 준비해서 그들이 '관광한국'의 주역이 되길 소망합니다. 동시에 그 주역이 되기 위해 철저하게 준비해야 함을 말하고 싶습니다. 그 준비 항목에서 빼 놓을 수 없는 첫 번째 것이 바로 외국어, 그 중에서도 영어입니다. 관광학도들의 실질적인 관광현장에서 사용할 수 있는 원만한 관광영어의 구사는 '관광한국' 달성의 결정적 역할을 할 것입니다.

Survival Tourism English! 이 한 권의 책이 목적의식과 열의를 가지고 준비하는 관광학도들에게 큰 힘이 되기를 바랍니다. 다른 것 보다 이 책은 체계적이고 꼼꼼한 관광현장영어를 접할 수 있다는 것과 풍부한 관광영어 참고자료를 싣고 있다는 것이 큰 장점입니다. 여기에는 이 시대 최고의 영어 선생인 천재윤 교수님의 열정적인 연구가 큰 몫을 했습니다. 감사드립니다.

아무쪼록 이 책을 접하는 모든 관광학도들이 수업현장에서 큰 만족을 얻고 관광영어 학습에 큰 성취감을 맛보기를 간절히 소망합니다. 미흡한 가운데서도 이 책의 집필을 인도하신 하나님께 감사를 드립니다.

서황골 연구실에서 저자 **문영수**

Preface

다변화되어가는 한국사회에서 영어가 필수가 된지 오랜 시간이 흘렀다. 각각의 사회구성원들은 그들의 목적에 맞는 영어를 습득하기 위해 온·오프라인에서 바쁘게 움직이고 있다. 이번에 출판되는 *Survival Tourism English*는 관광관련해서 필수적으로 알아야 할 표현을 정리함으로써 일반 영어학습자는 물론 해외여행자, 여행관련 업무 종사자 그리고 관광학도들에게 필수적인 책으로 자리매김을 할 것이다.

이번 책이 출판될 수 있도록 모든 집필과정에서 혼신의 노력을 기울이신 문영수 교수님께 진심으로 감사드린다. 이 책이 많은 독자층을 확보하거나 좋은 반응을 불러일으킨다면 그분의 노고임을 밝히는 바이다.

끝으로 항상 옆에서 큰 힘이 되어주는 사랑하는 가족과 대학, 어학원 제자들에게도 고마움을 표하고 싶다.

한해가 밝아오는 겨울 자락에
원어학원 연구실에서 저자 천재윤

Contents

I 영어회화 이 표현만큼은 알아둡시다.

01. Excuse me. 실례합니다. 죄송합니다.

02. You're welcome. 천만에요.

03. Excuse me? 미안합니다만, 그것은 무슨 뜻인지요?

04. I don't know. 글쎄요. 모르겠습니다.

05. How(are) you doing? 별일 없으세요? 어떻게 지내십니까?

06. Take care (of yourself). 건강하세요. 몸조심하세요.

07. Right. 맞습니다. 바로 그렇습니다.

08. I guess (so)./ I guess not.
~라고 생각합니다./ ~이 아니라고 생각합니다.

09. Sure. 물론이죠. 천만에요.

10. I'll be right there. 곧 그쪽으로 가겠습니다.

11. Thanks (a lot). 감사합니다. 고맙습니다. 고마운 일이라서.

12. Just a minute./ Just a sec(ond). 잠시만 기다리세요.

13. What's wrong? 뭐가 잘못됐나요?

14. Anytime. 천만에요. (돌아가는 손님에게) 언제라도 또 오세요.

15. Could I take a message? 메모를 남겨 드릴까요?

16. Guess what? 저어 있잖아?

17. Don't worry. 걱정 마세요.

18. Good luck! 행운을 빕니다. 힘껏 애써 봐.(야유조로)

19. How come? 어째서? 어쩐 일이에요?

20. Be careful! 조심해, 건강해!

21. Come (on) in. 들어오세요.

22. Help yourself. 편하게 쓰시지요. 어서 드세요.

23. Here (you are)./ Here you go. 여기 있습니다.

24. I doubt it./ I doubt that. 그럴까. 믿을 수 없어.

25. Never mind! 괜찮습니다. 마음 쓰지 마세요.

26. by the way ~하는 김에, 그런데

27. Have a good time./ Have fun. 즐겁게 지내세요.

28. Hopefully. 잘 되면. 운이 좋으면.

29. Hurry up! 서둘러!

30. I'll get it./ I'm coming! 내가 받을게요./ 내가 나갈게요.

31. What's the problem? (What seems to be the problem?)
무슨 일이야?

32. You've got to be kidding!/ You must be kidding.
설마 농담이겠지요.

33. (I) hope so./ (I) hope not.
~라면 좋겠는데. 그렇지 않았으면 좋겠어.

34. All right. 네, 좋습니다. 이제 됐어요.

35. Doing okay?/ You doing okay?
형편은 어떠세요? 순조롭게 잘 되세요?

Ⅱ 일상의 흔한 대화 연습

Bottoms up! 잔을 비워라!

술을 마실 때 잔을 단숨에 비우는 것은 'One shot'이 아니라 'Bottoms up'이다. '건배합시다'는 'Let's make a toast!'이다. 대개 'To your good health and happiness'(건강과 행복을 위하여)라고 하면서 건배한다. 잔을 부딪치면서는 'Cheers!' (건배)라고 한다. 술을 따를 때 상대방이 원하는 분량을 묻는 말은 'Say when'(어느 정도 따라 드릴까요)이다. 이때 원하는 만큼 잔이 채워졌으면 'When'(됐어요), 'Stop'(그만), 또는 'That's enough, thank you'(됐습니다. 고맙습니다.)라고 답한다. 누군가 초대했을 경우 주인은 항상 손님들에게 'Help yourself. Enjoy your meal'(마음껏 드십시오./맛있게 드십시오.)라고 한다.

A : OK, let's make a toast! To good health and happiness forever. Cheers! And bottoms up!
B : Cheers!

Just bring yourself! 그냥 오세요!

미국의 파티는 집주인이 모든 음식을 제공하는 공식적인 만찬(formal dinner parties)에서부터 손님 각자가 음식을 가지고 가는 편안한 모임(casual get- togethers)까지 매우 다양하다. 제각각 음식을 한 가지씩 만들어 와서 파티를 하는 potluck dinner, 야외에서 그릴에 고기와 소시지 등을 구워먹는 barbecue, 모든 음식을 큰 테이블에 두고 나누어 먹는 buffet supper가 있다. 또한 가벼운 알코올음료와 스낵이 제공되는 cocktail party와 레스토랑, 바 등에서 이른 저녁시간에 할인가격으로 술이나 스낵 등을 제공하는 happy hour 등이 있다. Potluck party에 초대를 받았을 때 What should I bring?이라고 묻는데 이때 아무 것도 가져올 필요가 없다고 얘기할 때 Just bring yourself라고 한다.

A : Would you like to come for dinner tonight?
(오늘 밤 저녁 하러 오실래요?)

B : Sure. I'd love to. Is it a potluck dinner? What should I bring?
(물론. 좋아요. 소찬파티 저녁인가요? 뭘 가져가죠?)

A : You don't need to bring anything. Just bring yourself. (뭘 가져올 필요 없어요. 몸만 오세요.)

I have a splitting headache. 머리가 몹시 아파요.

감기 증상 등으로 머리가 깨질 듯 아플 때 바로 이런 표현을 사용한다. 이외에도 감기 증상으로 표현할 수 있는 말들은 I have a runny nose(콧물이 흘러요), I have a stuffy nose(코가 막혀요), I have a fever(열이 있어요), I have a sore throat(목이 아파요), My voice is gone because of my cold(감기 때문에 목이 쉬었어요), I have a cough(기침이 나요), I ache all over(온몸이 아파요) 등이 있다.

A : What's the matter with you?
B : I feel terrible. I have a bad cold. I have a splitting headache, sore throat and a stuffy nose. So I can hardly breathe.
A : Oh, that's too bad. I hope it isn't serious. I think you'd better take a rest and drink a lot of fluid.

- **feel terrible** 몸이 너무 안 좋은
- **take a rest** 휴식을 취하다.
- **stuffy** 답답한, 숨 막히는
- **fluid** 수분, 물기

It's very G! 정말 잘했다, 멋져!

칭찬과 격려는 우리 생활 속에서 활력이 된다. 상대방 혹은 어떤 상황을 칭찬하고 격려하는 표현으로 'It's very G!' 가 있다. 여기에서 'G'는 'Great' 이나 'Good'를 축약한 것이다. 우리말로는 '좋아, 멋지군요' 혹은 '정말 잘했다, 멋져' 등으로 해석하면 무난하다.

A : I got a really nice job on my report card.
(성적이 잘 나왔어)
B : It's very G! (정말 잘했다, 멋져!)

❁ 이외에도 칭찬과 격려의 표현들을 조금 더 정리해 보자.
That's really good for a beginner. (초보자치고는 참 잘하네요)
Nice job on your report. (보고서 잘했어)
That was very good for your first time. (처음치곤 아주 잘했어요)

Money talks. 돈이 해결하지.

직역하면 '돈이 말한다'인데, 어찌 보면 어처구니없는 표현이다. 요즈음 사람들은 모든 일이 돈이 있으면 다 해결된다고 생각한다. 인간미의 풍요로움을 느끼기에는 너무 황금만능주의가 팽배해 있다. 그것을 빗대어 '돈이면 다 된다'라는 의미의 표현이다.

A : How can I do that? (어떻게 그것을 할 수 있죠?)
B : Money talks. (돈이 해결하지.)

❁ 이외에도 돈에 관련된 표현들을 조금 더 정리해 보자.
How much is it? (얼마죠?)
It's too much. (너무 비싸요.)
Could you come down a little? (좀 깎아 주실 수 있나요?)

After you. 먼저 하세요(타세요, 내리세요).

어떠한 일 앞에서 여러 사람이 순서를 기다릴 때 타인에게 먼저 하라는 표현이다. 흔히 '먼저 하세요' 인데 대중 교통수단을 이용할 때 이 표현은 '먼저 타세요' 혹은 '먼저 내리세요' 의 의미로 사용될 수 있다.

A : Are you getting off? (내리세요?)
B : After you. (먼저 내리세요.)

❁ 이외에도 교통에 관련된 유용한 표현들을 조금 더 정리해 보자.

Is this seat taken? 자리 있나요?
Which line goes downtown? 어떤 버스가 시내에 가죠?
Let me get off here. 여기서 내려주세요.

Should I fill it up? 가득 채워 드릴까요?

주요소에서 '가득 채워주세요' 하는 표현은 'Fill it up'이다. 예전에는 'Fill her up' 이란 표현을 주로 사용했지만, 요사이는 자동차를 여성명사로 받지 않고 중성명사로 간주해서 'it'으로 표현한다.

A : Should I fill it up? (가득 채워 드릴까요?)
B : No. Just give me five dollars worth, please.
(아뇨. 5달러어치만 넣어주세요.)
A : Okay. That's five dollars, please.
(알겠습니다. 5달러입니다.)
B : Here you are. (여기 있습니다.)

❁ 이외에도 '주유소'에 관련된 유용한 표현들을 조금 더 정리해 보자.

How often do you have to fill your car up? 얼마나 자주 기름을 넣죠?
How are you on gas? 기름은 어느 정도예요?
I'm running on empty. 기름이 바닥나간다.

I must be going now. 이제 가 봐야겠어.

누구와 만나서 얘기를 하는지 혹은 일을 하다가 또 다른 일을 위해서 그 장소를 떠나야 할 경우에 사용하는 표현이다.

A : I must be going now. (이제 가 봐야겠어.)
B : Thank you for visiting my house. (와 줘서 고마워.)

❁ 이외에도 위와 같은 상황에서 사용될 법한 유용한 표현들을 조금 더 정리해 보자.

Let's keep in touch. 연락하고 지내자.
Shall we meet again? 다시 만날까?
See you around. 잘 지내렴.
It's time you got going. 이제 갈 시간이다.
Drop me a line anytime. 언제든지 소식 주세요.

Can I tempt you? 한잔 할래?

인생을 재미있게 살려는 사람들에게 술은 큰 의미가 있다. 기쁠 때, 슬플 때, 우울할 때 함께하는 것이 술이다. 'tempt'는 '유혹하다'라는 의미를 갖고 있다. 물론 상황에 따라 달라질 수 있지만 위의 표현은 '한잔 할래?' 의 의미다.

A : Can I tempt you? (한잔 할래?)
B : Good idea. How about a glass of beer?
(좋아, 맥주 어때?)

❁ 이외에도 '술'에 관련된 유용한 표현들을 조금 더 정리해 보자.

How about one more drink? 한잔 더 하실래요?
He's a mean drinker. 그는 술주정이 심해.
I'm a slow drinker. 나는 천천히 마셔.
It's not strong enough. 독하지 않아.

My computer is frozen. 컴퓨터가 고장 났네.

현대인의 삶에서 컴퓨터가 없는 일상을 상상할 수 없다. 그러한 컴퓨터가 '얼었다'는 것은 '고장 났음'을 의미한다.

A : Can I come to your home and use the computer?
(당신 집에 가서 컴퓨터 좀 써도 될까요?)
B : My computer is frozen. (컴퓨터가 고장 났는데요.)

❁ 이외에도 컴퓨터와 관련되어 사용될 법한 유용한 표현들을 조금 더 정리해 보자.

The printer is out of paper. 프린터에 종이가 떨어졌어.
What computer did you save it on? 어디에다 저장했니?
What are those filed under? 그 파일들 어디에 있지?
Something is wrong with this disk. 이 디스크에 문제가 있어.

What is the exchange rate today?

오늘 환율이 얼마에요?

해외여행 중에 환전할 경우가 생긴다. 한 나라의 통화가 다른 나라의 통화로 교환되는 비율을 '환율'이라고 한다. 영어 표현으로는 'rate of exchange' 혹은 'exchange rate'이다. 보통 달러와 한화를 바꾸고자 할 때 1달러를 기준으로 하여, 'One dollar equals to 950 won(1달러 당 950원입니다)'이라고 표현한다.

A : Could you exchange these Korean won into US dollars? (이 한국 돈을 미화로 바꿔주세요?)
B : Sure. How much do you have?
(예. 얼마 가지고 계세요?)
A : It's 200,000 won. What is the exchange rate today?
(200,000원요. 오늘 환율이 얼마에요?)
B : The exchange rate today is 950 won.
(오늘 환율은 950원이에요.)

이외에도 환전과 관련된 유용한 표현들을 조금 더 정리해 본다.

How do you want the money? 돈을 어떻게 바꿔 내어 드릴까요?
Can I have change for twenty dollar bill?
20달러 지폐를 잔돈으로 바꿔 주실래요?

Would you tell me about your educational background? 학력에 대해 말씀해주시겠습니까?

요사이 대학생들은 전공(major)외에도 부전공(minor)을 많이 한다. 대학에서의 폭넓은 지식의 경험을 하고, 그 토대에 직장 선택의 길을 넓힐 수 있다. 취업 면접 시에 아래와 같은 대화가 오갈 수 있다.

A : Would you tell me about your educational background? (학력에 대해 말씀해 주시겠습니까?)
B : Sure, I attended Howon University.
(예, 호원대학교에 다녔습니다.)
A : What was major? (전공이 무엇이었습니까?)
B : I majored in Hotel Tourism with a minor in English. (호텔 관광학 전공에 부전공으로 영문학을 했습니다.)

❁ 이외에도 취업면접과 관련하여 학력에 관한 유용한 표현들을 조금 더 정리해 본다.

Can you use a word processor? 워드 프로세서를 사용할 줄 아십니까?
Can you make yourself understood in English?
영어로 의사소통을 할 수 있습니까?
Have you studied any other languages besides English?
영어 외 다른 언어를 공부한 적이 있습니까?

How long does the movie last?

상영시간은 얼마나 됩니까?

가을은 문화를 마음껏 누릴 수 있는 계절이다. 가까운 사람과 영화관을 찾는 것도 가장 손쉬운 문화 향유 방법이다. 이번에는 영화 관람에 관련된 표현들을 나눠 본다. 상영시간을 묻는 표현에서 'last' 대신에 'play'를 사용할 수 있다.

A : I'd like two tickets for The Shawshank Redemption.
("쇼생크 탈출" 영화표 두 장 주세요.)
B : Here you are. (여기 있습니다.)
A : How long does the movie last?
(상영시간은 얼마나 됩니까?)
B : It lasts two hours. (2시간 입니다.)

이외에도 영화 관람과 관련된 유용한 표현들을 조금 더 정리해 본다.

Are you a theatergoer? 영화 구경을 좋아하세요?
How often do you go to the movies? 영화는 얼마나 자주 보러 다니세요?
How much does the movie cost? 영화는 얼마입니까?
Who starred in the movie? 그 영화는 누가 주연했습니까?

Would you like to go to a party this Saturday? 이번 주 토요일에 있을 파티에 가시겠어요?

연말연시가 되면 각종 모임과 파티가 많이 생긴다. 그 중에 크리스마스 파티는 여러모로 기대가 되는 파티다. 파티에 관계되는 대화를 살펴본다.

A : Would you like to go to a party this Saturday?
(이번 주 토요일에 있을 파티에 가시겠어요?)
B : Sounds good. What kind of party?
(좋아요. 무슨 파티에요?)
A : It's Christmas Party with my family.
(저희 가족과 함께하는 크리스마스 파티에요.)
B : That's great. Thanks a lot. (멋져요. 너무 고마워요.)

❁ 이외에도 파티와 관련된 유용한 표현들을 조금 더 정리해 본다.
I'd like to invite you a party. 파티에 초대하고 싶습니다.
We're having a party next Friday. 다음 주 금요일에 파티가 있어요.
How many are coming for the party? 파티에 몇 사람이나 올 예정인가요?
You will come, if you like. 괜찮다면, 오세요.

No talking in class. 수업 시간에 떠들지 마세요.

대학생들도 강의 시간에 친구들과 잡담을 종종 한다. 교수님들에게는 무척 신경 쓰이는 일이다. 잡담하는 학생들을 향해 던질 수 있는 말이 오늘의 표현 'No talking in class'이다. 정확한 명령문은 아니지만 'No parking'처럼 명령문에 준해서 사용한다.

A : I'm not looking forward to this class. The professor is really strict.
(나는 이 수업 기대하지 않아. 교수님이 무척 깐깐하거든.)
B : Please be quiet!! (조용히 하세요!!)
A : I'm sorry, professor Lee. (이 교수님, 죄송합니다.)
B : No talking in class, or you will be asked to leave.
(수업 시간에 떠들지 마세요, 그렇지 않으면 퇴실시킬 겁니다.)

Note | 'look forward to+명사' 형태는 '~를 기대하다' 라는 뜻으로 사용된다. 마지막 문장은 '명령문+or' 구문으로 '~를 해라, 그렇지 않으면~'라는 뜻으로 해석 된다.

Why not take a family outing?

가족 나들이를 해보시는 게 어때요?

'To' 없는 부정사를 수반하여 'Why not~?'의 형태로 쓰일 경우에는 '~하면 좋지 않습니까?', '~하면 어떻습니까?', '~하지 않겠소?' 등의 의미를 나타낸다.

A : I'm visiting Korea with my family but we don't know what we should do here.
(가족과 함께 한국 방문 중인데요 무엇을 해야 할지 모르겠어요.)

B : Why not take a family outing?
(가족 나들이를 해보시는 게 어때요?)

A : That sounds great. Can you recommend a good place? (좋은 생각이군요. 좋은 곳을 추천해 주시겠어요?)

B : The zoo is a great place to have an outing.
(동물원이 나들이하기에 아주 좋습니다.)

Note | outing : 나들이, 소풍, 산책, 출장 / recommend : 추천하다

Let's get together again. 나중에 또 만납시다.

어떤 모임이나 회의를 갖고 헤어질 때 자주 사용하는 표현이 바로 'Let's get together again'이다. 이와 유사한 표현으로 'See you again', 'See you next time' 등을 들 수 있다. 대화 속에서 연습해 본다.

A : I really had a good time. Thanks for inviting me, Miran. (정말 재미있었어. 초대해 줘서 고맙다, 미란아.)
B : No problem, Sumi. I was glad you could come. (천만에, 수미. 네가 와 줘서 기뻤어.)
C : And I really enjoyed meeting you. (저도 만나서 정말 즐거웠어요.)
A : Likewise. Let's get together again. (저도 그래요. 나중에 또 만납시다.)

Note get together : 모이다, 만나다.
cf go together, meet together, work together.
have a good time : 재미있게 보내다(enjoy oneself).
No problem : 별것 아닙니다. 괜찮습니다. 천만에요.
Likewise : 마찬가지입니다(=Same here, me too).

Good jobs are hard to find.

좋은 직장을 얻기가 힘드네요.

2학기 말 즈음 되면 취업을 준비하는 사람들의 발걸음이 바빠진다. 취직을 하는데 요사이는 '외국어 능력'이 크게 좌우 한다. 취업에 좋은 소식이 오갔으면 한다.

A : Hi, Hyejin! How's your job search going? (안녕 혜진! 구직은 잘 되어가나요?)
B : I haven't had any luck so far. (아직은 행운이 따르지 않네요.)

A : Why not? There are a lot of companies hiring these days. (왜요? 요즘 채용하는 회사들이 많이 있는데요.)
B : That's true. There are many jobs. But....Good jobs are hard to find. (맞아요. 일자리가 많아요. 하지만....좋은 직장을 얻기가 힘드네요.)

Note How is .... going? ...이 잘 되어가다 / so far 아직까지는 / hire 고용하다 / these days 요즘

All leaves have already fallen!

나뭇잎들이 벌써 떨어졌어요!

한 학기가 마무리될 때 친구들과 헤어지면서 멋진 계절 인사를 나눠보면 어떨까?

A : It's chilly out here. (밖이 추워요.)
B : It sure is. Hey, look at the trees!
(어머, 정말이에요. 나무들 좀 봐요!)
A : All leaves have already fallen!
(나뭇잎들이 벌써 떨어졌어요!)
B : Yes, and it feels like winter is in the air.
(예, 바람은 겨울 같아요.)

Note chilly 추운, 쌀쌀한 / hey '어이, 어머나' 등의 기쁨, 놀람, 주의, 물음 등을 나타내는 말 / feel like ~ ...할 것 같다, ...일 것 같다

I've got a fever and I ache all over.

열이 나고 온 몸이 아파요.

신종 플루가 유행하고 있다. 자신의 건강에 이상이 있을 때 간략한 표현을 연습해 본다.

A : You look pale. What's wrong?
(얼굴이 안 좋아 보인다. 어디 아프니?)

B : I've got a fever and I ache all over.
(열이 나고 온 몸이 아파요.)

A : There's a new flu going around. You'd better see a doctor. (신종 플루가 유행하는데. 병원에 가 봐야겠어.)

B : I see. After that, I'll go home early and get some rest. (알았어요. 병원 들른 후 일찍 집에 가 쉬어야겠어요.)

Note | pale : 창백한 / fever : 열 / ache 통증, 통증을 느끼다 / flu : 'influenza', 독감 / get rest : 휴식을 취하다

Have you decided what you're going to major in? 어떤 전공을 할 건지 결정하셨나요?

새 학년 새 학기가 시작될 때 여러 인사말을 나눈다. 선택한 학교와 전공에 만족하는가? 이런 대화를 연습해 보자.

A : What university did you choose?
(어떤 대학을 선택하셨나요?)

B : I chose to attend Howon University.
(호원대학교에 가기로 정했어요.)

A : Excellent choice! Have you decided what you're going to major in?
(잘 선택했어요! 어떤 전공을 할 건지 결정하셨나요?)
B : I'm going to major in Hotel Tourism.
(호텔관광학을 전공하려구요.)

Useful expressions

What are you majoring in? 무엇을 전공하십니까?
I'm majoring in politics. 저는 정치학을 전공하고 있습니다.
My major is philosophy. 제 전공은 철학입니다.

Survival Tourism English

Ⅲ 관광영어 회화 연습

Section 1

Airline Service

Chapter 1. Check-In Service

Reservation

A : Asiana Airlines. May I help you, sir?

P : I have an open ticket for Chicago and I'd like to make a reservation for a flight to Chicago.

A : When would you like to leave?

P : By flight next Sunday.

A : Right. Hold on, please...., we have two flights at 9 a.m. and 4 p.m., what time would you like to make it?

P : At 4 p.m.

A : What class would you like?

P : Economy class.

A : All right. Your name and cell phone number, please?

P : My name is Young-soo Moon and 010-4654-9718.

A : O.K. Your reservation is booked for flight 320 to Chicago next Sunday at 4 p.m.

You can call me, if there is any change in the flight time.

P : That's all right. Thank you very much.

A : Don't forget your flight time.

➾ A : Airline agent　P : Passenger

Reconfirmation

P : Hello. This is Young-soo Moon. I'd like to reconfirm my reservation.

A : What reservation are you holding?

P : I've made a reservation for your flight 320 leaving tomorrow at 4 p.m. to Chicago.

A : How many are there in your party, sir?

P : Just one.

A : Hold on, please...., you're booked on our flight 320 to Chicago tomorrow.

Changing and Cancelling

A : Japan Airlines. May I help you sir?

P : Could you change my flight time for tonight at 9 o'clock to tomorrow at 4 p.m.
(I'd like to cancel my reservation for tonight.)

Ticketing

A : Good morning. May I help you, sir?

P : I'd like to purchase my ticket. I already have a reservation. My reservation number is AA 200.

A : Your name, please?

P : Young-soo Moon

A : Yes, sir. 2 p.m. Saturday, Asiana Airlines, right?

P : Right. How much is the fare?

A : It's $ 990 for round-trip.

P : Do you accept BC card?

A : Sure. May I have, please?

P : Here you are.

....

A : Would you like to sign here, please?

P : O.K.

A : Here is your ticket for Chicago, economy class, on Flight 005 leaving at 2 p.m. on October 14th.

Check-In

P : Is this right counter to check in for this flight?

A : Yes, it is. May I have your passport and ticket, please?

P : Here you are.

A : How many pieces of baggage do you have?

P : Two. I'd like a window seat.

A : Right, please put your baggage on this scale.

P : O.K. Is the plane on schedule?

A : Yes, it is. Please be present at the boarding gate 20 minutes before departure time.

➻ 탑승수속(Check-In)은 출국의 첫 번째 단계로서 승객이 좌석을 배정받고 수하물을 부친 후 탑승권을 받는 과정이다. 출국시 절차는 1. 탑승수속 2. 출국 일반 대합실 3. 보안 검색 4. 휴대물 검사 5. 출국심사 등이다.

Request of Boarding Station

P : Excuse me. I want to board OZ Flight 320 to Chicago. But is this the way to Gate 5?

C : Oh, it's. Go straight on and turn left.
You'll see a sign.

P : Thank you very much.

C : You hurry-up, please!

P : Passenger C : Crew

Chapter 2. Check-In Announcements

1. Announcement in the Airport

Flight OZ 411 to Los Angeles due to depart at 10:00 is now boarding at Gate 8.

2. Government Formalities for Departure

May I have your attention, please? Passengers who have not finished the formalities for departure are requested to come to the customs office immediately.

3. Check-In

May I have your attention, please? Passengers for Asiana Airlines Flight OZ 411 bound for Los Angeles departing at 10:30, please go through check-in and baggage check at Asiana check-in counter. Thank you.

4. Security Check-In

May I have your attention, please? Passengers for Korean Airline Flight KE 500 bound for Chicago at 12:30, please have your travel card and passport ready and proceed to the departure lounge. Thank you.

5. Departure Delayed

Your attention, please. Asiana Airlines announces the departure of Flight No. 320 for Chicago at 4 p.m. This Flight 320 bound for Chicago is now in its final boarding. Please proceed to the boarding gate.

.....................Asiana Airlines announces Flight No. 320 has been behind schedule.

6. Boarding

Your attention, please. Asiana Airlines announces the departure of Flight OZ 411 for Los Angeles. Those with first-class tickets, small children, or needing assistance please board at this time. Our staff is ready to assist you. We will call for other passengers in a few minutes. Thank you for flying Asiana Airlines today.

Economy class passengers holding boarding cards with seat numbers between rows 35 and 50 are requested to board now.

Chapter 3. ***Before Take-off Service English***

At the Boarding Station

S : May I help you find your seat?

P : Yes, please. Where is 27-H?

S : This way, please. Your seat is right over there by the window.

P : Thank you.

S : Would you show me your boarding pass, please?

T : Here you are.

S : It is right over there on the aisle.

T : By the way. I'd like a window seat.
May I change my seat.
S : That's not the case.

- That's not the case 그럴 수 없어요. 그러한 경우가 없어요.
- S : Stewardess P : Passenger T : Traveler

Announcements

Good afternoon. Ladies and gentlemen. We wish to welcome you aboard this flight ....

Please be certain your seatbelt is fastened and abstain from smoking until the No Smoking sign is turned off. Please press the call button if you need any help. Thanks.

Boarding-Conversation

P : A lovely day, Right?
T : It certainly is.
P : Excuse me, but could I have your name please?
T : It's John, John Smith.
P : Mr. Smith. My name is Young-soo Moon. I'm Korean. Nice to meet you. Are you British?
T : No. I'm American. Excuse me, what do you do for a living?

P : Professor and pastor.

T : Oh, Is that so? what is your purpose of going to Chicago?

P : To visit Moody Church and travel the country.

T : Well, nice to have met you. Hope you'll enjoy your stay in Chicago.

Seating Arrangements

P : May I sit here?

T : I'm afraid this seat is taken.

P : Oh, is it?

T : Yes, Why don't you ask the stewardess when she comes by? She should be able to help you find one.

....

P : I'd like to change my seat.

S : All Right. This way, please. We have lots of vacant seats at the window. I'm sure you'll be delighted with it.

P : Thank you.

Chapter 4. ***En-route Service English***

Beverage Service

S : Hello. What would you like to drink?
We have orange juice, coffee and wine.

P : Orange juice, please.

T : Excuse me, may I have something to drink?

S : Sure. What would you like?

T : What do you have?

S : We have complimentary coffee and alcoholic beverages. Here's a beverage list for other drinks.

T : I'd like to have a glass of whisky, please.

- complimentary coffee 기내에서 서비스로 제공하는 커피

Meal Service

S : Which would you prefer, steak or spiny lobster?

P : Spiny lobster, please.

....

S : Do you have finished your dinner, sir?

P : Yes, I enjoyed it very much.

S : What would you like for dessert, sir?
We have a choice of ice-cream or cake.

P : No, thank you. You see. I'm on a diet.

S : You'd like a cup of coffee or orange juice instead.

P : Coffee, please.

Newspaper Service

S : Would you like a paper?

P : Yes, please.

T : May I have a magazine or something?

S : Certainly. Just a moment. I'll be right back with one. Which do you prefer, one in Korean or English?

T : One in English, please.

S : All right, sir.

⇢ paper 신문(newspaper)

Blanket Service

P : Excuse me. Could I have a blanket?

S : I'm afraid there aren't any at the moment.
Can you wait just a little while?

P : O.K., I will.

S : I'll bring you one as soon as I find one available.

P : Would you, please? Thank you.

T : I'd like to have a nap. May I have one more blanket, please?

S : I'm sorry. Can you wait just a little while?

Sick Passenger

S : You look kind of pale. What's the matter?

P : I feel like vomiting.

S : Do you? Just a minute. Let me get the airsick bag ready. .... Here.

P : Thank you. Excuse me, do you have any medicine for a digestive?

S : All right, sir.

➾ vomit 토하다(throw out)

Facilities Service

P : Excuse me. How do I adjust the ventilation?

C : Please turn the knob, sir.

P : And how do I adjust the volume?

C : Just turn this dial, sir.

Do you know how to change channels?

P : I have no idea

C : Just turn this dial, sir.

P : Will you show me how I turn on and off the light?

C : Please push the switch that looks like a light bulb.

P : Where can I plug in the earphone?

C : Right here, sir.

P : I'm very sorry, but I have one more question.
How do I recline my seat and return it to the upright position?

C : Just push this button, lean back and lean forward.

P : Thank you very much.

➻ P : Passenger C : Cabin crew

In-flight Shopping 1

C : May I help you?

P : I'd like to buy neckties. Do you have Giantone Tie?

C : Yes, we have. How about this one?

P : I like it. How much do I owe you?

C : Twenty-five dollars, sir.

P : Can I pay by charge?

C : Of course.

➻ charge 신용카드(credit card)

In-flight Shopping 2

P : Would you show me some cosmetic, please?

C : Right. What brand do you want?

P : I want to buy some Christian Dior.

C : Hello. What are you looking for?

T : I want to buy some cigarettes.
What kind of cigarettes do you have?

C : We have Glory, Marboro, Sallem.....and so on.

T : I want Glory. Five packs, please.

Transit Passenger Announcement 1

Your attention, please. We shall be arriving in Anchorage after three minutes. Please make sure that seat belts are fastened, and extinguish all cigarettes. This plane will stay to Anchorage Airport an hour.

Transit Passenger and Transit Passenger Announcement 2

T : I'm changing flight. Are you changing flight, too?

P : No, I am not.

S : Are you a transit passenger?

P : Yes.

S : Please receive transit card.

Don't you leave anything valuable!

P : Right. What's the boarding time?

S : At 6:20 p.m.

Your attention, please. Transit passengers, Please wait at the lounge. The gate number for Northwest ....Airlines to Chicago is 10.

⊸ transit passenger 통과여객 혹은 경유 손님(주유나 기타 사정에 의해 경유지에서 기내 밖으로 나와 잠깐 쉬는 여행객)

Changing Flight

S : Are you a transit passenger, sir?

T : No. I'm changing flight.

S : What is your connecting flight?

T : I have to take a connecting flight to Atlanta.

Where can I confirm my flight?

S : Go to the Airlines desk, please.

Chapter 5. Check-Out Service English

Immigration 1

I : Hello. Your passport, please?

P : Here it is.

I : What's the purpose of your visit?

P : To travel the country.

I : How long are you staying in America?

P : For two weeks.

I : O.K. Go ahead and find your baggage, please.

P : Thank you.

Immigration 2

I : Hello. What's the purpose of your trip?

P : For Sightseeing.

I : How long will you be in the United states?

P : For two weeks.

I : Enjoy your trip.

P : Thank you.

I : Next, please. May I see your passport?

T : Here you are.

I : I see you are on a business visa.
How many are there in your party?

T : Just one.

Baggage Claim

P : Excuse me, but where is the baggage claim area?

W : Over there. Do you have your baggage check?

P : Yes, I have.

P : I can't find baggage. Will you please?

W : I'll try to find them.

P : Thank you.

Customs

C : Hello. Do you have your customs declaration form, please?

P : Here it is.

C : Are these all your bags?

P : Yes, they are. Here is my passport.

C : Thank you. Do you have anything to declare?

P : No, I don't. I only have personal effects.

C : Do you have any gifts, or valuable articles?

P : No, I don't.

C : Do you have more than five thousand dollars?

P : No.

C : Then, go through the green channel.

P : I see. Thank you.

입국시 절차는

1. 입국 심사 2. 보안 검색 3. 수하물 회수 4. 세관 검사
5. 입국 일반 대합실 등이다.

Chapter 6. ***Preparation for Return***

Reconfirmation

P : Hello. This is Young-soo Moon.
I'd like to reconfirm my reservation.

A : What reservation are you holding?

P : I've made a reservation for your flight 156 leaving tomorrow at 2 p.m to Seoul.

A : How many are there in your party, sir?

P : Just one.

A : Hold on, please..., you're booked on our flight 156 to Seoul tomorrow.

P : passenger A : Airline agent

Seeing Off

A : Here we are at the airport.

P : It's very nice of you to see me off.

A : My pleasure. I hope you have a nice trip.

P : I am very grateful to you for your kind hospitality during my stay here. I'd better go and check in at the counter. Good-bye.

Checking-In

A : May I have your passport and ticket, please?

P : Here you are.

A : How many pieces of baggage do you have?

P : Two. I'd like a window seat.

A : Right, please put your baggage on this scale.

Boarding Station

P : Excuse me. I want to board OZ Flight 156 to Seoul. But is this the way to Gate 7?

A : Oh, it's. Go straight on and turn left.

P : Thank you very much.

Announcement

Your attention, please. Asiana Airlines announces the departure of Flight No. 156 for Seoul at 2 p.m. This Flight 156 bound for Seoul is now in its final boarding. Please proceed to the boarding gate.

Section 2

Hotel Service

Chapter 1. ***Check-In***

B : May I help you with your baggage?

P : Please. Where can I register?

B : Come this way, please.

Front Desk 1

P : Hello. I'd like to check in. My name is Young-soo Moon and I have a reservation for a single room with bath.

C : Oh, yes. Mr. Moon. We have your reservation. Would you fill out this registration form, please?

P : O.K. Will this do?

C : Fine. You are in room 1517. Here is your key. I'll call a bellman to carry up your baggage.

Bellman

B : Are these all your bags?

P : Yes, they are.

B : Right this way. Well, here we are. This is your room.

P : It's very nice room.

B : If you need more assistance, call me.

P : O.K. Thank you for your help.

B : You're welcome. Enjoy your stay.

Front Desk 2

P : Excuse me, but where is the reception desk?

D : At the front desk over there to your left, sir.

C : Good evening. Do you have a reservation?

P : Sure. I made a reservation in Seoul.
My name is Young-soo Moon.

C : Right. Will you fill in this registration form, please?

P : Here you are.

C : Fine. You are in room 1112. Here is your key.

P : O.K. Thank you for your help,

Reservation 1

R : Hilton Hotel. May I help you?

P : Hello. I don't have a hotel reservation and just arrived at the airport. I want to reserve a double room with bath for this evening. Do you have?

R : Yes, we have.

P : What's the room rate?

R : Thirty dollars a night including tax.

P : O.K., I'll take the room. My name is Young-soo Moon. At the hotel by six o'clock.

Reservation 2

P : Good morning. I arrived without reservation a hotel. Do you have a twin room for tonight?

R : Are you going to stay here just for tonight?

P : Yes.

R : I'm sorry. We are full tonight.

P : Can you suggest another hotel?

Reservation 3

P : Hello. This is Young-soo Moon. I'd like to confirm my reservation.

R : What reservation are you holding?

P : I've reserved a double room for three nights.

R : Hold on, please……, We have your reservation.

Without Reservation 1

P : Can I have a room, please?

W : Yes, we have a nice room on the third floor.

P : How much is it?

W : Twenty dollars per night, plus tax and service charge.

P : May I see the room?

W : Sure. Come this way, please.

P : Take this room, please.

Without Reservation 2

P : Hello. I want a room, please.

W : What kind of room would you like?

P : I'd like a twin room with a nice view.

W : All right. sir. We have one good room vacant on

the second floor. How long will you be staying here?

P : Three nights.

W : Right this way. Well, here we are. This is your room.

P : It's very nice room.

W : If you need more assistance, call me.

Without Reservation 3

P : Do you have a double room?

W : Yes, How long will you be staying here?

P : Two nights. What is the room rate?

W : Twenty-five dollars per night.

P : Does it include the tax and service charge?

W : Sure.

P : How much is it?

W : About fifteen percent.

Check-In : Expressions

Do you have a room available?

How much does the room cost?

A cheap and clean room, please.

Is breakfast included in the charge?

Will you please have my baggage taken up to my room?

Where is the security box?

Where is the closet for my clothes?

Is there anything cheaper?

I'd like to confirm my reservation.

Chapter 2. Room Service

Wake-up Call

O : Operator.

P : Hello. I'd like a wake-up call, please.

O : For what time?

P : 6 o'clock(6 a.m), please.

O : What is your room number?

P : Fifteen seventeen.

O : O.K. Good night.

P : Thank you.

Room Service-Meal 1

W : Room service.

P : I'd like to order breakfast, please.

W : Sir. What would you like?

P : Two ham and eggs, toast and coffee.

W : All right, sir. I'll send it up right away.
What is your room number?

P : Fifteen seventeen.

Room Service-Meal 2

W : Good morning. How are you?

P : I'm fine, thank you.

W : Would you like to have breakfast now?

P : Yes, please. I'll have an American Breakfast.

W : O.K. How would you like your eggs?

P : Scrambled, please.

Room Service-Transportation and Laundry

P : Hello. Room service? This is room fifteen seventeen. please call me a taxi.

W : All right, sir. That'll arrive about ten minutes.

P : You can call me, if they arrive in front of this hotel.

W : Sure..

......

P : Laundry service? I'd like to have two shirts washed.

L: Yes. I'll come up and by them. What's your room number?

P : Fifteen sixteen. Can I have them back by evening?

L: Yes. Around 6 o'clock, sir.

P : Thank you.

Room Service-Expressions

I'd like to order a snack, please.

May we have breakfast in our room?

I'm still waiting for breakfast I ordered.

I'd like to have my laundry.

I want my shirts cleaned.

I'd like to have two shirts ironed. (pressed)

I'd like to have necktie dry cleaned.

When will they be ready?

Chapter 3. ***Check-Out***

P : Hello. This is in room fifteen seventeen.
Please send someone to bring down my baggage.

F : Are you checking out, sir?

P : Yes. I'll be right down. Would you please have my bill ready?

At the Front Desk

F : That will be one hundred and twenty-five dollars. Can you pay by cash or credit card?

P : By the way. May I pay by traveler's check?

F : Yes, you may.

P : My stay in your hotel has been very pleasant.

F : Thank you for staying with us, sir.

P : Good bye.

Leaving a Hotel

P : Good evening, I'll check out tomorrow morning about 8.

F : All right, sir. Your name and room number, please?

P : My name is Moon, fifteen sixteen.

F : O.K. We'll have your bill ready.

[Next Morning]

P : How much is the total bill?

F : That will be one hundred dollars. ($100.)

P : I'd like to pay for that with traveler's check.

F : Fine. I'm looking forward to seeing you again.

P : I'll try. Good bye.

Chapter 4. ***Hotel Restaurant***

Reservation 1

P : Hello! I'd like to make a reservation for dinner.

W : Certainly, sir. When would you like to go?

P : Tonight, please.

W : For how many people?

P : For Five. How much will this cost?

W : Twenty dollars per person.

P : O.K. That's all.

W : Yes, we can. Thank you for calling.
See you later, sir.

Reservation 2

P : Hello, Lady's Restaurant?
I'd like to reserve a table at 7 this evening.

W : We're booked up that time.
Could you make it at 7 : 30?

P : All right. we can. We'll be there at 7 : 30.
Can I wear casual clothes?

W : Yes. sir. What's your name?

P : The name is Moon.

W : Right. Thank you for calling.

Reservation 3

P : I have a reservation. The name is Moon.

W : Good evening, sir. Please come this way.

Wine

W : What would you like to drink wine, sir? We have Chablis. Moselle, California and Bordeaux wine.

P : Chablis wine, please.

W : Yes, sir.

....

P : Your Chablis wine. Would you like me to pour the wine?

W : Yes, please.

Cocktail/ Beer

P : May I have the cocktail list, please?

W : Yes, sir. We have dry sherry, whisky soda, gin tonic scotch water, and strawberry.

P : Give me a glass of strawberry, please.

W : O.K. Just a moment, please.

Waiter!……

W : Did you call me? May I help you, sir?

T : What kind of beer do you have?

W : We have a Miller and Stout.

T : Give me a bottle of Stout

Giving an Order 1

W : Are you ready to order now, sir?

P : Oh yes, We'll have two beef steaks, please.

W : Yes, sir. How would you like your steaks?

P : Well-done for the lady and medium for myself.
Also can we have a combination salad?

W : Yes, you can. What kind of dressing would you like?

P : Thousand island, please.

W : O.K. Thank you.

Giving an Order 2

W : Do you have finished your dinner, sir?

P : Yes, I enjoyed it very much.

W : What would you like for dessert, sir?
We have a choice of ice-cream or coffee.

P : Coffee, please.

Giving an Order 3

P : Hello. Any tables available?

W : Please wait here for a few minutes.

......

W : Now we have a table for you. Please come this way.

P : Would you show me the menu, please?

W : Here you are. Would you like to order now, sir?

P : What's today's special menu?

W : We have Salmon with Smoked dish.

P : Salmon with Smoked dish, please.

......

W : And you, sir?

T : I'd like to order a light meal.
Do you have ham sandwich?

W : Yes, sir. What would you like to drink?
We have orange juice, and coffee.

T : Orange juice, please.

W : Thank you very much.

Giving an Order 4

W : Good morning, sir.
What would you like for breakfast?

P : I'm fine, thank you. I'd like a piece of bread and coffee.

American Breakfast

W : And you, sir?

T : Two ham and eggs, bacon and coffee, please.

W : How would you like your eggs?

T : Sunny-side-up, please.

W : Thank you.

Giving an Order 5

P : Two hamburgers and one big hot dog, please.

W : For here or to go, sir?

P : To go, please.

W : What would you like on your hamburgers?

P : Sliced tomatoes, please.

W : Here you are.

That'll be three dollars fifty cents.($3.50)

Giving an Order 6

W : What would you like to drink, sir?

P : Give me a glass of Brandy, please.

W : All right, sir.

.....

P : Another one, please.

W : What would you like, sir?

T : Scotch on the rocks, please.

At the Counter

P : Waiter! check, please.

C : That'll be twenty-five dollars.
May you pay by cash or credit card?

P : Can I pay by traveler's check?

C : Yes, you may.

P : I enjoyed it. Thank you very much.

Section 3

Tour Guide

Chapter 1. Transportation and Communication

Taxi 1

D : Where to, sir?

P : I'd like to go to Central Park.

D : Yes, sir. Are you in a hurry?

P : Yes, I must be there by one o'clock. I have an appointment with one of my American friend.

....

D : Here we are, sir.

P : How much do I owe you?

D : Eleven dollars.

P : Here you are. Keep the change, please.

D : Thank you.

Taxi 2

D : Where are you going, sir?

P : Downtown, please.

D : All right, sir. What part of downtown are you going?

P : Mall street, please.

D : Yes, sir.

P : But I want to stop at the Chicago building for a few minutes. How long does it take to go to Chicago building?

D : About thirty minutes. There is very much traffic.

Renting a Car 1

P : Hi. I'd like to rent a car for two weeks.

C : What kind would you like?

P : An economy car, a compact.

C : May I see your international driver's license?

P : Yes, here it is.

C : Just fill out this form. Unlimited mileage and the mandatory collision insurance are included.

P : Do I have to return the car to this location?

C : No. You can drop it off at any of our local branches.

P : I see. Where is your car now?

C : It's in the parking lot.

Renting a Car 2

P : I'd like to rent a car, please.

C : What kind would you like?

P : A small automatic, please.

C : May I see your international driver's license?

P : Yes, here it is.

C : How long do you want it for?

P : Four days. What is the rate?

C : Twenty-five dollars per day with unlimited mileage.

Car Maintenance

Can you send a breakdown tow car?

The engine doesn't start.

Where's the nearest garage?

My car broke down on the highway.

Send someone for it.

How long will it take to fix it?

Gas Station

P : Fill it up with regular, please.

W : All right, sir.

P : Please check the water in the radiator.

W : The radiator's all right.

Where is the gas station?/

I've run out of gasoline./

Check the oil, please.

Bus 1

P : Does this bus stop at the downtown?

D : Yes. Get on, please.

P : How much is the fare?

D : Thirty cents.

P : I'm going to get off at Mall Department Store.

Will you tell me when to get off?

D : Certainly.

Bus 2

P : Excuse me. Does this bus go to town center?

D : Yes, it does.

P : I want to go to the Mall Plaza.

How many stop from here is it.

D : The fifth stop.

P : Thank you.

Bus 3

P : I'm going to get off at Hyde Park.
How many stop from here is it?

D : You are on the wrong bus.
Get off at the next stop and take bus number five.

Bus 4

P : I'd like to go to Chicago. Give me one ticket, please.

C : Is that one way or round trip?

P : One way ticket. What's the fare to Chicago?

C : 17 dollars.

P : Right. One ticket, please.

C : Here is your ticket.

P : Thank you very much.

Bus 5

Where is the bus stop?

What time will the next bus leave?

I get off at the next stop.

How many stops is it from here?

How often does the bus come?

Please let me know when we get there.

Where is the ticket office?

Do you have any medicine good for carsickness?

Train 1

P : I'd like to go to Gunsan. Is there an express train?

C : There is a 10:40 express.

P : When is the next train?

C : It leaves at 11:40

P : I'll take it. How much is the fare to Gunsan ?

C : That will be twenty dollars.

P : Right. One ticket, please.

Train 2

Where's the booking office?

I want to reserve a seat on this train.

I'd like to reserve a berth. Up berth, please.

May I cancel this ticket?

I lost my ticket.

What time does the train arrive in Chicago?

Is this seat taken?

I lost my briefcase on this platform just a little while ago.

➾ berth 침대칸 / up berth 침대칸 위층

Subway

P : Excuse me. Can I go to Central Park by subway?

C : Yes, sir.

P : What's subway fare to Central Park?

C : The minimum fare is nineteen cents.

P : A one-way ticket, please. Where is the entrance?

C : Sure. Go straight ahead and you'll come right to it.

P : Thank you.

.....

P : How many train stop to Central Park?

W : The fifth stop.

Sea Transportation

P : Hello. I'd like to reserve a deck chair.
How much is the fare to Mount Vernon.

C : Ten dollars thirty cents.

P : What time do we board?

C : At 11 a.m.

P : I feel like seasick.
Do you have any medicine good for sea sickness?

Airmail

C : May I help you?

P : How much does it cost to send a letter to Korea by airmail?

C : 45 cents if you use an aerogram, it's 39 cents.

P : I see.
I'd like five 45-cent stamps, and three aerograms.

C : That'll be three dollars and forty-tow cents.

P : Here's five dollar bill.

C : O.K. Here you are. And here's your change.

Post Office 1

P : This letter needs to go by registered mail.

C : Where is it going?

P : To the Howon company.

C : Fill out this from and sign at the bottom.

P : Here you are.

C : O.K. That is 20 cents for the stamp and two dollars to send it by registered mail.

Post Office 2

P : I'd like to send this package to Korea by air.

C : What's in it?

P : They are all personal goods.
Will you wrap this as a parcel?

C : Right. Would you fill out this form, please?

P : Will this do?

C : O.K. That is 80 cents for the stamp and thirty dollars to send it by parcel.

Collect Call

O : Operator. May I help you?

P : Hello. I would like to make a collect call, please.

O : What's the number and party's name?

P : Young-Soo Moon, 063-450-7443.

O : I need your name and room number, please

P : This is Young-soo Moon fifteen seventeen.

O : Hang up and I'll call back.

P : Hello. This is Young-soo Moon fifteen seventeen.

O : Go ahead. Your party's on the line.

Phone Call 1

W : Good morning. Howon University.

P : Hello May I speak to Prof. Moon, please?

W : I'm sorry, Prof. Moon is in a meeting at the moment. Can he call you back?

P : Sure.

W : May I have your name and number, please?

P : Right. This is Jae-yun Cheon. I'm at 715-9064.

W : I'll have him call you right back.

Phone Call 2

W : Good morning. May I help you?

P : I'd like to speak to Mr. Cheon, please.

W : Sorry, he is off today.

P : I see. Do you know if he will be back in the office tomorrow?

W : He won't be back tomorrow. He is on vacation.

P : I'll call back later on.

Phone Call 3

P : Hello. Is Mr. Cheon in?

W : Sorry. Mr. Cheon just stepped away from his desk.

P : When will he be back?

W : I'm sorry, but I have no idea.
May I take a message?

P : Yes. Would you ask him to call Mr. Cheon?

W : Right. Thank you for calling.

P : You're welcome.

Phone Call 4

P : Hello. Is this the Cheon's residence?

W : Yes.

P : This is Young-soo Moon.
May I speak to Mr. Cheon, please?

W : Yes, Hold on, I'll get him.

P : Thank you.

[잠시 후....]

P : Hello. This is Mr. Moon. I was wondering if you'd like to go out to dinner tonight?

T : That would be nice. What time should we meet?

P : Around 7. Is it too late for you?

T : No. I'll be ready!

Phone Call 5

W : Hello. Is Mr. Moon there?

M : There's no one here by that name.
You have the wrong number.

W : I'm sorry to have bothered you.

M : That's all right.

Phone Call 6

Let me tell you my new phone number.

Hold on, please. I'll get a pencil.

I can't hear you. Would you speak more loudly?

Could you repeat that, please?

May I ask what this is in reference to?

(무슨 일인지 여쭤 봐도 될까요?)

Where is a public phone?

The line is busy.

Please call me up tomorrow morning.

Let me call you back later.

He will be back in a few minutes.

May I leave a message for him?

Would you answer the phone when it rings?

Chapter 2. Shopping and Exchange

Shopping 1

P : Excuse me. Could I have this one?

W : Just a moment, please. I'll be with you in a second.

P : I'd like to buy this camera.

W : You made an excellent selection.

This is the largest selling brand.

P : How much is it?

W : One hundred and twenty dollars.
Can you pay by cash or credit card?

P : By the way. May I pay by credit card?

W : Yes, you may.

Shopping 2

T : Please show me the one in the window?

W : What can I show you?

T : Would you show me that watch?

W : This one? How about this one?

T : O.K. I'll take it.

W : It is twenty dollars.

Shopping 3

W : What are you looking for?

P : No, thank you. I'm just looking around.

W : Yes, sir.

P : Excuse me. Would you show me this one?

W : This one? Purple bags are very popular this year.

P : Is it made of real leather?

W : Yes, it is.

P : How much is it?

W : Sixty dollars.

P : It's too expensive. Please show me a cheaper one.

W : O.K. How about this one?

P : (I don't like it.) I'll be back again.

Shopping 4

C : What are you looking for?

W : Excuse me. May I try this skirt on?

C : Oh, sure. The fitting room is right over here.

W : Thank you.

C : How does it fit?

W : It's little too tight. May I have a medium?

C : Right. I'll get it for you.

[A little later...]

W : Isn't the skirt a bit too long?

C : Yes. You look beautiful.

W : O.K. I'll take it. How much is it?

C : One hundred and thirty dollars.
Can you pay by cash or credit card?

W : Traveler's check, please.

C : Fine. Sign it here.

Shopping 5

W : May I help you?

P : I'd like to see one of those ties.

W : You mean this one?

P : Yes.

W : It's pretty, isn't it?

It's made of pure silk and is on sale.

P : O.K. I'll take it. Will you gift-wrap it, please?

W : Could you take it to that counter, please?

Shopping 6

P : Do you carry perfume here?

W : We sure do. Which brand do you want?

P : I'd like to buy some Lotus Eau.

W : Yes, I'll get it for you.

P : O.K. I'll take it. How much is it?

W : Twenty dollars.

(잠시 옆 손님에게)

W : Hello. What are you looking for?

T : I'd like to buy a Guerlain Compact.

W : Over here, sir.

T : Fine. I'll take it. Please put it in a bag.

Shopping 7

W : How much is this Scotch?

C : Twenty dollars and sixth cents.

W : Can I pay by check?

C : I'm afraid you can't.
We accept only traveler's checks and credit cards.

W : O.K. How about this card then?

P : We can take it. Please sign here.

Shopping 8

P : Do you carry books of poetry?

W : We sure do.
What kind of poems are you interested in?

P : I like poems that tell us something.

W : Well, in that case I'd recommend the once on Shelf K-3 over there.

P : I'll take these two.

W : Thank you. I'll wrap up the books for you.
I hope you'll enjoy reading them.

Shopping 9

P : Excuse me. I bought this just now and here's the receipt. I'm afraid I was short-changed. Could you look into it?

W : Oh, really?.......Sorry, here's the five I owe you. I'm terribly sorry.

Exchange 1

C : May I help you, sir?

P : Yes. I'd like to cash this travelers check.

C : How much would you like to cash?

P : Seventy dollars, please.

C : How do you want the money?

P : Twenty dollar bill, four tenners, two quarters, three dimes, and four nickels.

C : Right. Sign it, please.

Exchange 2

C : May I help you, sir?

P : Yes. Can I have change for two dollar bill?

C : Sure.

P : Five quarters, six dimes, and three nickels, please.

C : Next, please. Good Morning, sir?

T : Would you please change some dollar bills?

C : Yes, sir. How do you want the money?

T : Small change, please.

Chapter 3. Sightseeing

Sightseeing Information 1

W : Good morning. May I help you?

P : I'd like to see some of city's sights.
Do you have any tour to Chicago?

W : Sure. Are you taking a tour today?

P : Yes. How much is it per person?

W : Twenty-five dollars.

Sightseeing Information 2

W : Have you seen much of Disneyland?

P : Yes.

W : Did you go to the National Museum, too?

P : I did. There were lots of things to see.
I might go there again before I leave.

W : Good idea. What else did you see?

P : I saw a folk dance at the National Theater the other night.

W : How did you like that?

P : Very much. It was a wonderful show.

Balloon Riding

P : Excuse me. Sorry to bother you, but could you tell me where I can buy ticket for balloon riding?

W : Go to Box C on the third floor.

P : I'd like two tickets for the next balloon ride, please.

C : The tickets for the 2:30 flight are all sold out, and the next flight will be at 3:30.
Will that be all right?

P : O.K. Balloon riding must be very popular.

C : It's getting more and more popular.
Here are your tickets. That'll be four dollars.

P : O.K. Here you are.

C : Have a good time.

P : Thank you.

Sightseeing Expressions

I'd like to get a city map, please.

Do you have any sightseeing program?

Is lunch included?

I'd like to see some of the city's nightfall.

Do you have any tour to Disneyland?

Do you have a sightseeing brochure?

I'm going to see New York on my own.

What's that building over there?

I'd like to see some places of interest.

Do you know what that is?

Do you know where I can go and return in a day?

Taking a Picture 1

P : Excuse me. Would you please take our picture?

W : Sure. Where would you like to stand?

P : Stand right here, please.
You may just push the button.

W : O.K. Smile. Good.

P : Thank you very much.

Taking a Picture 2

P : Excuse me. May I take a picture of you with your children?

W : Sure.

P : Smile....Cheese!.....I'll mail it to you.
Tell me your address please.

W : Thank you. I hope it comes out good.

Taking a Picture - Expressions

I need a roll of film for my camera.

Will you take our picture?

I want you to join us, if you don't mind.

Can you focus the camera?

I need to develop my negatives.

How much do you charge for developing?

This camera doesn't work. Can you repair it?

Chapter 4. ***Directions***

Directions 1

P : Excuse me. The fact is I'm lost.
Could tell me the way to the Mall Center?

W : Sure. Just go straight along this street and turn right at the next corner.

P : How long will that take?

W : Oh, only a few minutes.

P : Thanks a lot.

Directions 2

P : We're completely lost. Where are we now?

W : I'm sorry. I'm a stranger here.

P : Here comes an officer. Let's ask him. Excuse me.
May I ask where we're now?

O : Yes, you're right in the middle of fifth Avenue.

P : Please point out where I am on this map:

O : All right.

Directions 3

P : Excuse me.
Can you direct me to the toy department, please?

W : It's on the 5th floor. As you get off the elevator, you'll see it on your right.

P : Can you direct me to the elevator?

W : Sure. Go straight ahead and you'll come left to it.

P : Thank you very much.

Directions 4 - Expressions

Which way to the hotel?

How long will it take me to get there?

Could you draw me a sketch, please?

How long does it take on foot?

Where do you want to go?

How far is it from here?

Where can I find a police box?

Is it in this direction?

Excuse me. Can you tell me where the rest room is?

Is it on the left or right?

Turn left at the end of the hall.

It's three blocks straight ahead. You can't miss it.

Chapter 5. *Amusement*

Movie

W : Go straight along this street.
The movie theater is opposite from the post office.

....

C : Hello. May I help you?

P : What films are on now?

C : Action movie.

P : What's the admission price?

C : Seven dollars. What kind of seats do you like?

P : I want a front seat, please.

Theater

P : What's on tonight?

W : We have Spider woman play.

P : What time does the curtain go up?

W : At 7 o'clock.

Concert

P : I'd like to buy an advance ticket for the concert by the Moscow Symphony Orchestra.

W : What kind of seats do you like?

P : I want a seat in the gallery.

Expressions

Where can I see an opera?

Are today's tickets still available?

Where can I get a ticket?

Would you like to go to the concert?

Can I have a seat for today?

How much are the tickets?

Could you tell me what musical is playing today?

Can you recommend a film?

Which film is popular?

Let's go to the movies tonight.

Chapter 6. ***Leisure and Sports***

Watching a Game

P : I'd like to see a basket-ball game. Can I still get a ticket?

W : Sure

P : What's the admission price?

W : Five dollars. What kind of seats do you like?

P : I want a front seat, please.

Swimming

P : Excuse me. What time does the swimming pool close?

W : At 5 o'clock. Did you bring your bathing suit?

P : Yes. How deep is the pool?

W : It's not too deep.

Jet-Skiing

P : I'd like to rent this jet skis. How much is it?

W : Five dollars.

P : I've never tried one. Can you teach me how to drive?

W : Sure. Just a moment, please.

Expressions

I want some information about basket-ball games.

Where can I get a ticket?

Is it possible to ski at this time of the year?

Lend me a fishing tackle, please.

How much must I pay per hour?

I don't have a reservation. Can we play some golf?

Do you have your own clubs?

How much is the green fee?

Chapter 7. Crisis Management

Illness 1

D : Sorry I kept you waiting. I'm Dr. Kram.

P : Good afternoon. Dr. Kram. I've heard a lot about you. People are speaking highly you.

D : Are they? I'm glad to hear that.
Well, what's the trouble?

P : I have a bad headache, and a sore throat, too.

D : Let me see. It's a bad cold. Nothing serious, though.

P : Am I going to be all right soon?

D : You'll be all right by Wednesday, I think.
Now the nurse will give you a shot and some pills.

P : Thank you very much.

D : Take care, Moon.

Illness 2

D : Well, what's the trouble?

P : I have a stomachache.

D : Nothing serious, though.
I'll prescribe some medicine for your stomach.

P : Thank you very much.

(잠시 후...)

P : Some stomach medicine, please.

D : Do you have the prescription?

P : Yes, I have.

Illness 3

D : What's the matter?

P : I've got a pain in my ankle.

D : Nothing is the matter with the bone.

P : Thank you very much.

How's your appetite.

Give me a peptic, please.

Take me to the hospital, please.

Accident 1

P : I lost my traveler's checks.

C : Did you remember where you lose them?

P : I was not sure.

C : Do you have the record with the check numbers.

P : Yes. Here it is. When can I have them reissued?

C : Just a moment, please.

Accident 2

W : What can I do for you?

P : I lost my bag on this platform just a little while ago.

W : What kind of bag is it?

P : It's brown bag.

W : How can we contact you, if we find your bag?

Expressions

Where is lost and found office?

Where should I come to get it?

Could you please look for it?

Where shall we send it for you, if we find it?

I lost my passport.

Where did you lose it?

Please reissue my passport.

Where did you put it?

I left my bag in the taxi.

Appendices

부록 *1.* ***A Resume***

A resume tells about your education. It also tells about your work experience and skill.

1. Read about Moon, Ji-yun.

"Hello. I'm Moon, Ji–yun. I live at 34189 Ocean Street, Seattle, Washington 18101. My phone number is 206–555–1011. I'm 20 years old. I was born May 7, (year). I graduated from Lincoln High School three years ago. Then I started at Seattle Community College. I'm studying Travel and Tourism. I will graduate next May. I have a part–time job at the Palace Hotel. I'm a front desk clerk. I can use a computer and am good at word processing(60 wpm–words per minute). I speak two foreign languageS : Mandarin Chinese(intermediate) and Spanish(elementary)."

Moon Ji–yun
34189______________________________
_________, ____________________________
Phone: ____________________
Date of Birth: __________________

Employment objective

To work for a travel company

Education

College :

Seattle Community College

MajoR : Travel and Tourism

September, ____________ to present

Will graduate ________________

High School :

____

Graduated, June ______

Work Experience

1997 to present

____________________, ______________________,

Seattle(part time)

Special skills :

____________ skills

Good __________________ ability(_____wpm)

Languages :

Mandarin Chinese(___________)

______________________(elementary)

References on request

2. Now, write your resume.

3. A "letter of application" is the letter you send with a resume. When you apply for a job, you may have to write a letter of application. Do you know how to write one? Write a letter of application. This is a example below.

January 14 (year)

Personnel Director
Howon Travel
138 Warren Ave.
Seattle, Washington 18112

Dear sir or madam :

I am applying for the position of travel agent which was advertised in the Seattle Post of January 13.

I am enclosing my resume. As you can see, I will graduate from Seattle Community College next May. My major is Travel and Tourism. I can use a computer and speak chinese and some Spanish.

I would appreciate the opportunity for an interview.

I look forward to hearing from you.

Sincerely,

Ji-yun Moon

enc.

부록 2. 인천 공항 이용 항공사 코드

IATA	ICAO	영어명	항공사명(국적)	국적
AC	ACA	Air Canada	에어 캐나다	캐나다
AD	PRZ	Air Paradise	에어 파라다이스	인도네시아
AF	AFR	Air France	에어 프랑스	프랑스
AI	AIC	Air India	에어 인디아	인도
B7	UIA	UniAir	유니항공	대만
BC	SKY	Skymark Airlines	스카이마크항공	일본
BR	EVA	Eva Air	에바항공	대만
CA	CCA	Air China	중국국제항공	중국
CI	CAL	China Airlines	중화항공	대만
CV	CLX	Cargolux Airlines	카고룩스항공	룩셈부르크
CX	CPA	Cathay Pacific Airways	캐세이퍼시픽항공	중국
CZ	CSN	China Southern Airlines	중국남방항공	중국
EF	FEA	FarEastern Air Transport	원동항공	대만
EK	UAE	Emirates	에미레이트항공	아랍에미레이트
FM	CSH	Shanghai Airlines	상하이항공	중국
FX	FDX	Federal Express	페더럴익스프레스	미국
GR	GCO	Gemini Air Cargo	제미나이항공	미국
H8	KHB	Dalavia Airlines	달라비아항공	러시아
HU	CHH	ChinaHainan Airlines	중국해남항공	중국

IATA	ICAO	영어명	항공사명(국적)	국적
HY	UZB	Uzbekistan Airways	우즈베키스탄항공	우즈베키스탄
HZ	SHU	Shkalinsk Airlines	사할린항공	러시아
IR	IRA	Iran Air	이란항공	이란
JL	JAL	Japan Airlines	일본항공	일본
JT	LNI	Lion Air	라이언항공	인도네시아
K4	CKS	Kalitta Air	칼리타항공	미국
K9	KRI	Eurasia Airlines	크릴로항공	러시아
KE	KAL	Korean Air	대한항공	한국
KL	KLM	KLM Royal Dutch Airlines	네덜란드항공	네덜란드
KZ	NCA	Nippon Cargo Airlines	일본화물항공	일본
LD	AHK	Air Hongkong	에어홍콩	중국
LH	DLH	Lufthansa	루프트한자항공	독일
LY	ELY	Israel Airlines	이스라엘항공	이스라엘
MF	XMN	Xiamen Air	중국샤먼항공	중국
MH	MAS	Malaysia Airlines	말레이시아항공	말레이시아
MU	CES	China Eastern Airlines	중국동방항공	중국
NH	ANA	All Nippon Airways	전일본공수	일본
NW	NWA	Northwest Airlines	노스웨스트항공	미국
NX	AMU	Air Macau	에어마카오	중국
OM	MGL	Mongolian Airlines	몽골항공	몽골
OX	OEA	Orient Thai Airlines	오리엔트타이항공	태국
OZ	AAR	Asiana Airlines	아시아나항공	한국

IATA	ICAO	영어명	항공사명(국적)	국적
P7	ESL	Eastline Airlines	이스트라인항공	러시아
PO	PAC	Polar Air Cargo	폴라에어카고	미국
PR	PAL	Philippine Airlines	필리핀항공	필리핀
QR	QTR	Qatar Airlines	카타르항공	카타르
SC	CDG	Sandong Airlines	산동항공	중국
SQ	SIA	Singapore Airlines	싱가포르항공	싱가포르
SU	AFL	Aeroflot Russian Int'l Airlines	아에로플로트항공	러시아
TG	THA	Thai Airways	타이항공	태국
TK	THY	Turkish Airlines	터키항공	터키
UA	UAL	United Airlines	유나이티드항공	미국
VN	HVN	Vietnam Airlines	베트남항공	베트남
WI	TDX	Trade Winds Airlines	트레이드윈즈항공	미국
XF	VLK	Vladivostok Air	블라디보스톡항공	러시아
4L	KZR	Air Astana	에어 아스타나	카자흐스탄
5J	CEB	Cebu Pacific Air	세부퍼시픽항공	필리핀
5X	UPS	UPS Airlines	유피에스항공	미국
5Y	GTI	Atlas Airlines	아틀라스항공	미국
7B	KJC	Krasnoyarsk Airlines	크라스노야르스크항공	러시아
91	TKY	Thai Sky Airlies	타이스카이항공	태국
9R	VAP	Phuket Air	푸켓항공	태국
9S	SOO	Southern Air	미국남부화물항공	미국
	NVI	Avial NV	아비알NV	러시아

부록 3. *An Itinerary*

An itinerary is a travel plan. Ji-yun took a tour to Cairns, australia. Look at her itinerary. What questions could you ask about her trip? Finish the questions.

ADVENTURE TOURS

Cairns Tour Itinerary

Saturday, 8/19

10:30 a.m. Arrival, World Airways, Flight 821,

Was your plane on time?

Cairns Airport, International Terminal.

Will be met by Adventure Tour Guide.

11:30 a.m. Bus tour of city and surrounding area.

2:30 p.m. Deliver to hotel ________ *the hotel like?*

Sunday, 8/20

8:30 a.m. Hotel pick-up. Boat to Green Island.

Swimming,

________ *the weather?*

snorkeling and scuba diving.

________ *go scuba diving?*

(Barbecue lunch provided.)

6:30 p.m. Return to hotel.

Monday, 8/21

9:00–11:30 a.m. Hotel pick–up. Visit Wild World Animal Park.

What animals __________ ?

12:00 noon Return to hotel. Afternoon free for shopping.

______ *you buy* ______ ?

Bungee jumping optional.

______ *your try* ______ ?

Tuesday, 8/22

8:00 a.m. Hotel pick–up. Escorted trip into rain forest.

______ *rain forest like?*

(Guide and 4WD vehicle provided.)

7:30 p.m. Return to hotel.

Wednesday, 8/23

7:45 a.m. Hotel pick–up. Transport to airport, International Terminal.

11:15 a.m. Departure, World Airways 823.

______ *sad to leave?*

2. Think about a trip you took. Write the itinerary.

■ Here are some items in room service menu of a hotel below. Check it out!

부록 4. A La Carte Lunch And Dinner

A La Carte Lunch And Dinner

점심·저녁식사/ご昼食、ご夕食、深夜

11a.m. ~ 6a.m.

Appetizers

19 Walker Hill Smoked Salmon ₩14,000
Home Smoked Salmon with Horseradish and Capers
Served with Melba toast
훈제연어 / スモークサーモン

20 Shrimps Salad with Melon ₩10,000
Green Pepper corn dressing
새우샐러드와 메론 / 海老サラダとメロン

20. *Shrimps Salad with Melon*

21 Chef's Salad ₩15,000
Julienne of Ham, Cheese, Chicken, Roastbeef on a bed of crisp Lettuce served with your favourite Dressing
주방장 특제 샐러드 / 料理長特製のサラダ

22 Garden Salad ₩6,000
Array of seasonal Salads with your choice of Dressing
계절 샐러드 / フレッシュサラダ

Soups

23 Double Beef Consomme with Vegetables ₩6,000
소고기 맑은 수프 / 牛コンソメスープ

24 Hungarian style Goulash Soup ₩7,000
헝가리식 소고기 수프 / ハンガリー式牛スープ

25 Cream of Corn Soup with Crabmeat ₩6,500
게살 옥수수 크림 스프/かにとコーンクリームスープ

26 Traditional French Onion Soup ₩6,500
Gratinated with Gruyere Cheese
프랑스식 양파 수프 / フランス式オニオンスープ

MAIN DISHES

30 **Chicken in the Basket** ₩15,000

Deepfried Chicken pieces served with Shoestring Potatoes,
And Cole Slaw Salad
닭튀김과 감자튀김/フライドチキンとポテトフライ

31 **Pork Cutlet** ₩15,000

돈까스/豚ガス

32 **Deepfried Prawns** ₩22,000

Accompanied by Shoestring Potatoes and Chilli Sauce
새우튀김과 감자튀김/海老とポテトのフライ

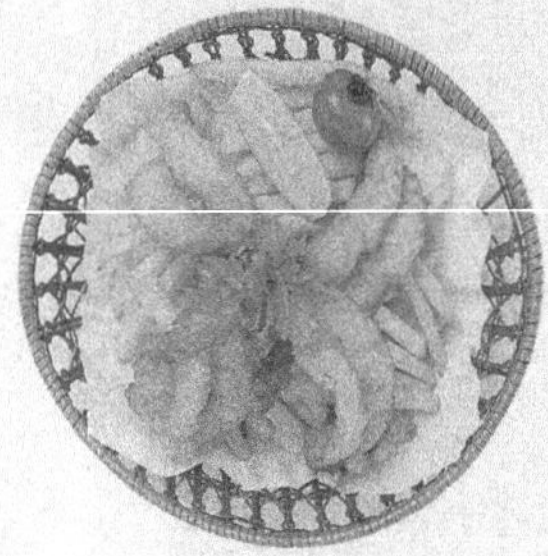

32. Deepfried Prawns

33 **Salisbury Steak with Mushroom Sauce** ₩18,000

Ground Beef patty served with buttered Noodles
And Vegetables
햄버거 스테이크 양송이소오스/
ハンバーガーステーキとマッシュルームソース

34 **Broiled Rib Eye Steak** ₩22,000

Accompanied by Red Wine Sauce
소고기갈비살스테이크와 적포도주소오스
牛ヒレステーキとレッドワインソース

35 **U.S. Sirloin Steak** ₩22,000

Served with Herb Butter
소고기등심스테이크와 향료버터/サーロインステーキとハーブバター

36 **Black Pepper Fillet Steak** ₩26,000

소고기안심 후추스테이크/牛肉のペッパーステーキ

36. Black Pepper Fillet Steak

Oriental Dishes

44 **Chinese Fried Rice** ₩15,000

Choice of Shrimps, Beef or Chicken

중국식 볶음밥(새우, 소고기 또는 닭고기)
中国風チャーハン(海老、牛肉または鶏肉)

45 **Tempura U-Dong** ₩18,000

Japanese Noodles in Broth – with fried Shrimp,
And dried Seaweed

일본식 튀김우동/日本風天ぷらうどん

46 **Omelette Rice** ₩15,000

Rice with diced Beef and Vegetable cubes
Wrapped in a thin Egg omelette

오므라이스/オムライス

47 **Beef Curry** ₩17,000

Served with Steamed Rice

소고기 카레라이스/ビーフカレー

48 **Grilled Abalone with Garlic Sauce** Current

Served with Steamed Rice and Seasonal Vegetables

전복구이와 마늘소스 /焼きあわびとガーリックソース

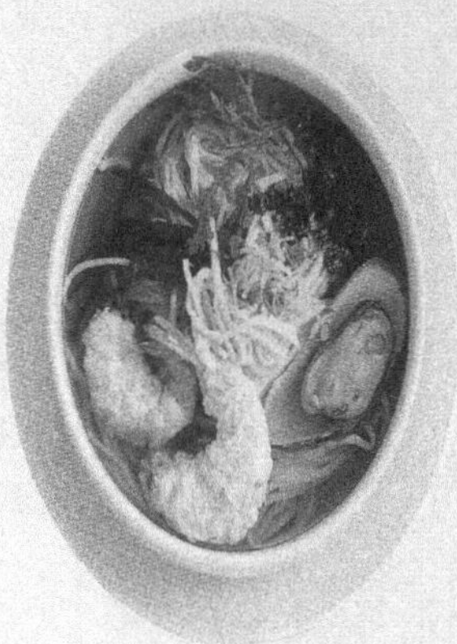

45. Tempura U-Dong

48. Grilled Abalone with Garlic Sauce

DESSERTS

51. White Chocolate Parfait

51 **White Chocolate Parfait with Redwine Pear** ₩5,500
쵸코렛 파페/チョコレートパーペ

52 **Kardinal Pastry with Vanilla-Coffee Sauce** ₩5,500
모카 페스트리/モカペストリ

53 **Apple Pie with Sour Cherry Ice Cream** ₩5,500
사과파이와 체리아이스크림/アップルパイとチェリアイスクリーム

54 **Selection of Daily Cakes, Pies, French Pastries** ₩5,500
프랑스식 양과자 / フランス風洋菓子

55 **Ice Cream** ₩5,500
Two Scoops of Vanilla-, Strawberry-, Chocolate-, Nougat-, Ice Cream
Topped with whipped Cream
아이스크림선택 / アイスクリーム

BEVERAGES

56 **Freshly brewed Coffee** ₩5,000
커피 / コーヒー

57 **Sanka, Decaffeinated Coffee** ₩5,000
상카커피 / サンカコーヒー

58 **Lipton Tea, Earl Grey Tea, Darjeeling Tea** ₩5,000
홍차 / 紅茶

59 **Ginseng Tea with Honey** ₩5,000
인삼차와 꿀 / 高麗人蔘茶とはちみつ

60 **Green Tea** ₩5,000
녹차 / 緑茶

61 **Hot Chocolate** ₩5,000
핫 초코렛 / ホットチョコレート

62 **Ovomaltine** ₩5,000
오버말틴 / オボーマルティン

63 **Fresh Milk, Low Fat Milk** ₩5,000
Hot or Cold
각종우유 선택 / 各種牛乳

부록 *5.* 출입국신고서

〈출입국 신고서(E/D card의 예)〉

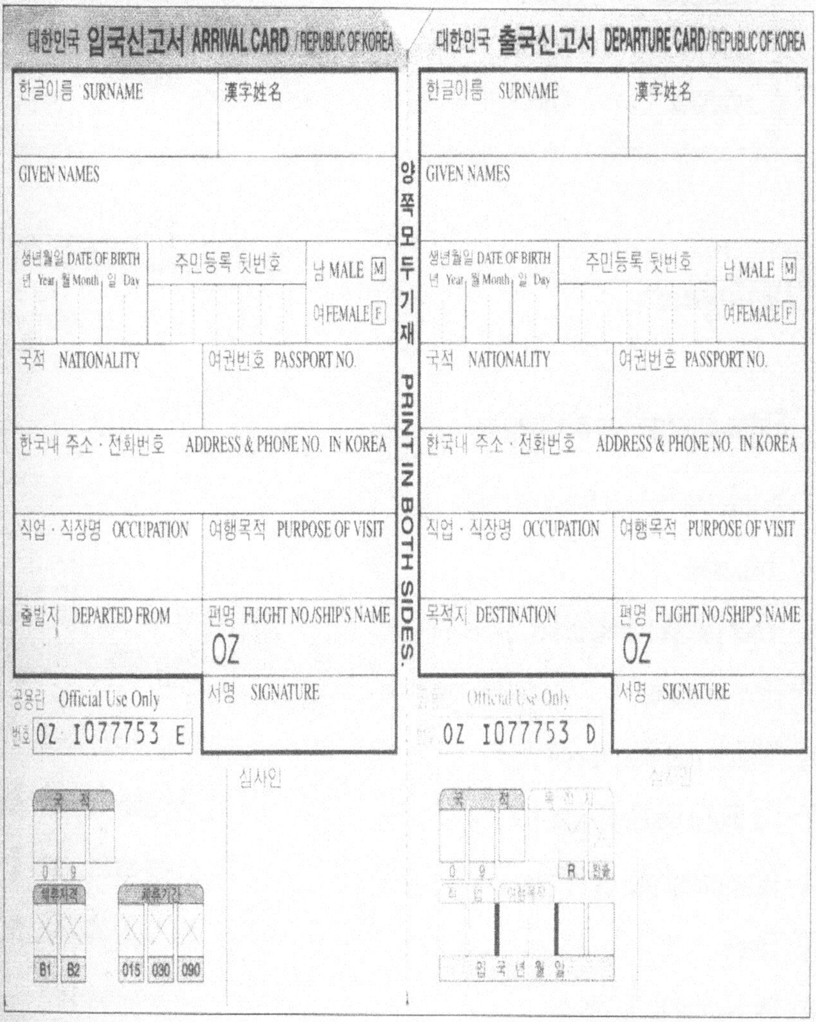

대한민국 입국신고서 ARRIVAL CARD / REPUBLIC OF KOREA

한글이름 SURNAME | 漢字姓名

GIVEN NAMES

생년월일 DATE OF BIRTH 년 Year 월 Month 일 Day | 주민등록 뒷번호 | 남 MALE M 여 FEMALE F

국적 NATIONALITY | 여권번호 PASSPORT NO.

한국내 주소 · 전화번호 ADDRESS & PHONE NO. IN KOREA

직업 · 직장명 OCCUPATION | 여행목적 PURPOSE OF VISIT

출발지 DEPARTED FROM | 편명 FLIGHT NO./SHIP'S NAME OZ

공용란 Official Use Only | 서명 SIGNATURE

번호 OZ I077753 E

심사인

국적 0 9

체류자격 B1 B2

체류기간 015 030 090

양쪽 모두 기재 PRINT IN BOTH SIDES.

대한민국 출국신고서 DEPARTURE CARD / REPUBLIC OF KOREA

한글이름 SURNAME | 漢字姓名

GIVEN NAMES

생년월일 DATE OF BIRTH 년 Year 월 Month 일 Day | 주민등록 뒷번호 | 남 MALE M 여 FEMALE F

국적 NATIONALITY | 여권번호 PASSPORT NO.

한국내 주소 · 전화번호 ADDRESS & PHONE NO. IN KOREA

직업 · 직장명 OCCUPATION | 여행목적 PURPOSE OF VISIT

목적지 DESTINATION | 편명 FLIGHT NO./SHIP'S NAME OZ

공용란 Official Use Only | 서명 SIGNATURE

OZ I077753 D

심사인

국적 0 9 | 목적지 R

입국년월일

부록 6. 세계시차표

세계 시차표 / World Time Zones

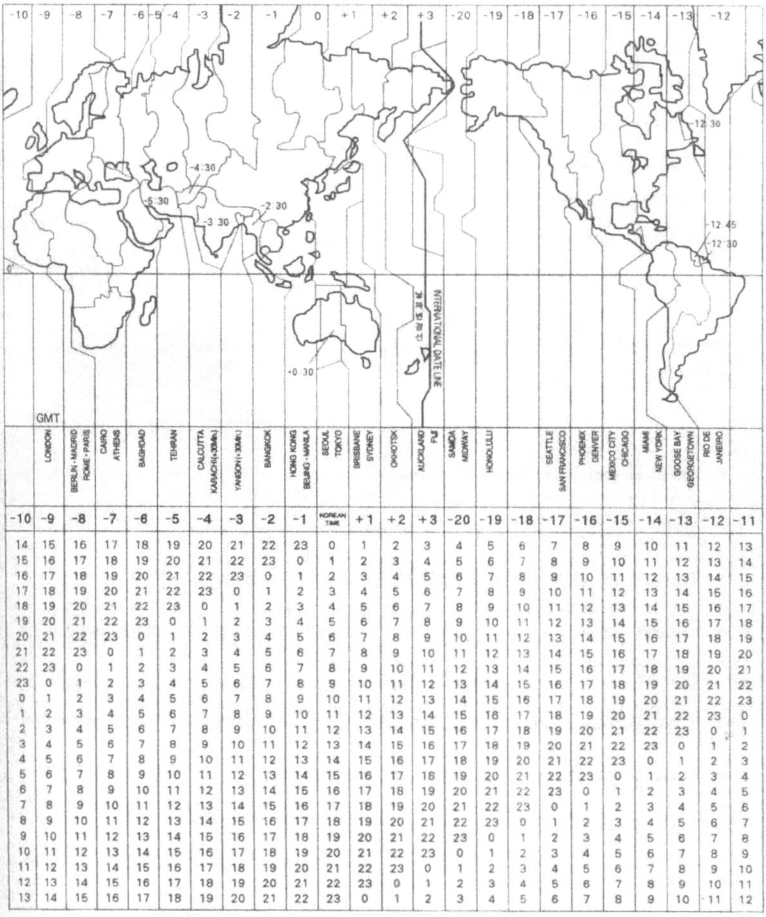

	LONDON	BERLIN · MADRID ROME · PARIS	CAIRO ATHENS	BAGHDAD	TEHRAN	CALCUTTA KARACHI(+30Min.)	YANGON(+30Min.)	BANGKOK	HONG KONG BEIJING · MANILA	SEOUL TOKYO	BRISBANE SYDNEY	OKHOTSK	AUCKLAND FIJI	SAMOA MIDWAY	HONOLULU		SEATTLE SAN FRANCISCO	PHOENIX DENVER	MEXICO CITY CHICAGO	MIAMI NEW YORK	GOOSE BAY GEORGETOWN	RIO DE JANEIRO	
-10	-9	-8	-7	-6	-5	-4	-3	-2	-1	KOREAN TIME	+1	+2	+3	-20	-19	-18	-17	-16	-15	-14	-13	-12	-11
14	15	16	17	18	19	20	21	22	23	0	1	2	3	4	5	6	7	8	9	10	11	12	13
15	16	17	18	19	20	21	22	23	0	1	2	3	4	5	6	7	8	9	10	11	12	13	14
16	17	18	19	20	21	22	23	0	1	2	3	4	5	6	7	8	9	10	11	12	13	14	15
17	18	19	20	21	22	23	0	1	2	3	4	5	6	7	8	9	10	11	12	13	14	15	16
18	19	20	21	22	23	0	1	2	3	4	5	6	7	8	9	10	11	12	13	14	15	16	17
19	20	21	22	23	0	1	2	3	4	5	6	7	8	9	10	11	12	13	14	15	16	17	18
20	21	22	23	0	1	2	3	4	5	6	7	8	9	10	11	12	13	14	15	16	17	18	19
21	22	23	0	1	2	3	4	5	6	7	8	9	10	11	12	13	14	15	16	17	18	19	20
22	23	0	1	2	3	4	5	6	7	8	9	10	11	12	13	14	15	16	17	18	19	20	21
23	0	1	2	3	4	5	6	7	8	9	10	11	12	13	14	15	16	17	18	19	20	21	22
0	1	2	3	4	5	6	7	8	9	10	11	12	13	14	15	16	17	18	19	20	21	22	23
1	2	3	4	5	6	7	8	9	10	11	12	13	14	15	16	17	18	19	20	21	22	23	0
2	3	4	5	6	7	8	9	10	11	12	13	14	15	16	17	18	19	20	21	22	23	0	1
3	4	5	6	7	8	9	10	11	12	13	14	15	16	17	18	19	20	21	22	23	0	1	2
4	5	6	7	8	9	10	11	12	13	14	15	16	17	18	19	20	21	22	23	0	1	2	3
5	6	7	8	9	10	11	12	13	14	15	16	17	18	19	20	21	22	23	0	1	2	3	4
6	7	8	9	10	11	12	13	14	15	16	17	18	19	20	21	22	23	0	1	2	3	4	5
7	8	9	10	11	12	13	14	15	16	17	18	19	20	21	22	23	0	1	2	3	4	5	6
8	9	10	11	12	13	14	15	16	17	18	19	20	21	22	23	0	1	2	3	4	5	6	7
9	10	11	12	13	14	15	16	17	18	19	20	21	22	23	0	1	2	3	4	5	6	7	8
10	11	12	13	14	15	16	17	18	19	20	21	22	23	0	1	2	3	4	5	6	7	8	9
11	12	13	14	15	16	17	18	19	20	21	22	23	0	1	2	3	4	5	6	7	8	9	10
12	13	14	15	16	17	18	19	20	21	22	23	0	1	2	3	4	5	6	7	8	9	10	11
13	14	15	16	17	18	19	20	21	22	23	0	1	2	3	4	5	6	7	8	9	10	11	12

부록 7. *Terminology*

A	
A.O.C	브로드와인의 원산지 관리증명
A La Carte	일품요리 메뉴 중에서 자기가 좋아하는 요리를 주문하는 형식
Accommodation	숙박시설, 편의시설. 호텔과 모텔 등의 보통의 숙박시설
Account	회계의 총칭
Additional Charge	추가요금
Advance Deposit	객실요금을 미리 지불하는 것. 선불
Advance Ticket	예매권(항공)
Age	증류주의 숙성과정에서 술통에 저장한 기간.Cf) vintage
Agent	여행대리점, 항공권 판매 대리점
Air Shooter	회계전표 자동수신기
Air Cargo	항공 화물
Air Carrier	항공사
Aircrew	항공사 승무원
Airport Hotel	이른 비행기를 탑승하는 사람들을 위해 공항근처에 있는 호텔. Airtel.
Airport Tax	공항세. 국가별로 차이가 있으나 대략 5,000에서 20,000원 내이다.
Ale	보통 맥주보다 고온에서 발효시킨 것. LagerBeer보다 호프량이 강함
American Breakfast	ConditionalBreakfast에 계란요리가 곁들인 조식

Aperitif Wine	식욕촉진을 위하여 전채요리와 함께 마시거나 식전에 제공되는 와인
Arcade	호텔연쇄가, 호텔의 상점 (보통 1층이나 지하에 있음)
Area Code	전화의 시외 국번
Arm Towel	종사원이 팔에 걸쳐 사용하는 서비스용 냅킨
Attendant	동반자
Audit	회계감사
Available	유효한, 가능한, 유용한
Average Room Rate	평균 일일 객실. 객실수입/총판매 객실수

B	
Baggage	수화물, 짐(luggage)
Baggage Claim	수화물을 찾는 장소
Banquet	연회 혹은 호텔 연회장
Bartender	호텔이나 레스토랑 등지에서 고객을 대상으로 식음료를 칵테일하여 판매하는 종업원
Bath Towel	목욕을 하고 난 뒤 닦는 목욕타올. 얼굴타올, 손타올, 발타올.
Bed And Board	아메리칸 스타일의 요금제도로서 객실요금에 3식이 포함됨
Behind Schedule	예정보다 지연된
Bell ManBoy	프런트에서 등록을 마친 후 객실까지 숙박객의 짐을 들고 안내하는 호텔 종사원
Beverage	음료.
BGM	호텔이나 백화점 등지에서 방문객이나 투숙객을 대상으로 들려주는 음악

Bidet	특급호텔 등의 스위트 객실의 욕실에 주로 설치되어 있는 위생용 세척기
Bill	호텔의 객실이나 식음료 상품을 이용함에 따라 발생하는 고객의 영수증
Blanket	객실 침대 위에 덮여져 있는 담요
Blended	한 가지 이상의 주류에 중화곡주를 혼합하는 것을 말함
Boarding Pass	탑승권
Boiled Eggs	삶은 계란
Booking	예약, 예약기록, 티켓의 발매
Bound For	~행(발)
Brochure	안내용 인쇄물
Brunch	아침식사와 점심식사의 중간에 먹는 메뉴로서 주로 10-12 사이에 제공되는 간단한 음식
Bulkhead	격벽, 첫 번째 좌석, 비상구 옆
Business Class	비지니스석
Business Hotel	주로 비즈니스 목적을 띤 고객을 대상으로 하는 호텔이며, 도심지에 위치해 있다

C	
Cab	택시
Cabin	객실
Cafeteria	음식물을 손님 자신이 날라다 먹기 편리하도록 카운터 테이블에 있어 직접 요금을 지급하고 이용하는 self service 식의 간이식당
Captain	업장에서 웨이터나 웨이트레스들을 통솔하며, 어떤 한 section을 담당하여 주문을 받는 주임급 직원

Carafe	하우스 와인을 담아서 제공하는 통
Carry-on Baggage	기내 휴대품
Cashier	회계원
Chamber Maid	Room Maid로 객실의 청소와 정돈을 맡은 여자종업원
Check-in	투숙절차를 밟는 것(호텔), 탑승 수속 과정(항공)
Check-out	퇴숙절차를 밟는 것(호텔), 입국 수속(항공)
Check-out Hour	고객이 객실을 비워야 하거나 하루의 추가요금이 부과되는 시간한계를 말하며 일반적으로 12시를 기준으로 한다
Check-out Time	숙박객이 퇴숙당일날 객실을 비워 주는 시간. 통상 12시
Civil Aviation Bureau	CAB, 민간 항공국
Claim Tag	화물을 맡겼을 때의 짐표(인환증)
Collect Call	수신자 부담
Commission	수수료
Complimentary Room	무료로 제공되는 객실
Concierge	유럽 호텔에서 볼 수 있는 용어로 호텔 외부에 관한 정보를 고객의 필요에 따라 제공하는 책임을 가진 자
Condiment	조리에 쓰이는 각종 양념류의 총칭
Conference	회의
Confirmation	고객이 도착하기 전에 예약사항을 확인하는 것
Continental Breakfast	쥬스, 토스트, 롤, 커피(차, 우유)로 구성된 아침식사
Convention	국제회의, 협의회, 대회, 협약

Cuisine	요리
Customs	세관
Cutlet	얇게 저민 고기나 생선에 밀가루, 계란, 빵가루 등을 묻혀서 구운 요리

D	
D.N.P (Direct Not Post)	게시판에 부착하지 마시오
Day Excursion	당일 돌아오는 여행
Day Rate	주간에 객실을 이용하는 고객에 대한 요금
Decanter	각종 음료를 담는 용기로서 칵테일 혹은 와인 Decanter가 있다
Demi Pension	숙박요금제도의 하나, 실료에 조식, 점심, 석식 중 2식을 포함
Dice	아주 작게 자른 야채 명칭
Discount	할인
Disembarkation Card	입국카드
Domestic Flight	국내선
Door Man	현관 앞에 드나드는 차량에 대한 대리 parking 업무와 자동차의 호출, 체크인하는 고객의 영접 및 굿바이 서비스를 행하는 호텔의 종사원
Double Bed Room	2명이 이용하는 한 객실 (때로는 TwinBed Room도 포함)
Double Double Room	2개의DoubleBed가 있는 객실
Draft Beer	생맥주를 말하며 제조과정에서 발효균을 살균하지 않은 생맥주(LagerBeer)
Drapery	커튼 안쪽의 주름 잡힌 것

Drug Store	호텔 내에서 간단한 잡화류를 파는 곳 또는 약국
Duty Free Allowance	면세로 반출입할 수 있는 양
Duty Free Shop	면세 물품 판매점

E	
Early Check-in	아침 일찍 호텔에 투숙하는 고객
Early Out	당초 예약한 날짜보다 일찍 퇴숙하는 것
Efficiency	부엌기능을 갖춘 숙박시설
Embarkation Card	EC, 출국카드
Emergency Exit	비상구
Entree	주요리로 제공될 수 있는 육류
Equipment	식당, 주방 및 연회행사에 필요한 각종 장비
Espresso	이탈리아식 커피 추출법으로 농도를 진하게 추출해 내는 방법
ETA	Estimated Time toArrival. 도착예정시간
ETD	Estimated Time toDeparture. 출발예정시간
Event Order	연회행사를 각 관련부서에 알리는 연회행사 통보서
Exchange	환전, 교환　Cf)Exchange rate 환율
Excursion	1~2일의 짧은 여행
Exit	비상구. 호텔의 각 층 양 끝에 파란 간판으로 표시되어 있음
Extension	숙박의 연장. 전화내선(구내전화)
ExtraBed	보조침대
Extra Charge	지정된 요금 외의 요금. 인원이 추가되거나 침대가 추가되는 경우 별도의 요금을 부과함
Eye Mask	수면을 위한 눈가리개

F	
F & B	Food & Beverage. 식료, 음료를 통칭하는 말
FIT	ForeignIndependent(Individual) Tour의 약어. 개인여행객
Family Plan	반드시 부모와 같이 같은 객실을 사용할 때 14세 미만의 어린이에게 적용하며, 침대는 엑스트라로 넣어주고 요금은 징수하지 않는다
Fare	철도, 항공, 해운, 공원 등의 공공요금
Filet	육류나 생선의 뼈나 지방질을 추려낸 상태
Finger Bowl	식사중 혹은 후에 손을 간단히 씻어내는 그릇으로서 레몬과 꽃잎 조각을 띄워서 제공한다
Flat Rate	균일요금을 말하며, 단체가 호텔에 숙박하는 경우 요금이 다른 객실을 사용하는 일도 있지만, 그것을 균일화한 특별요금
Flat Ware	테이블에 쓰이는 은기물류의 총칭
Flight Attendant	승무원
Floor Clerk	각 층에서FrontClerk의 여러 임무와 직능을 함께 수행하는 직원
Folio	고객이 투숙하는 동안 일어났던 모든 거래 관계를 적어 놓는 서식
Follow Up	재확인하다. 여행 후의 서비스
Forwarding Address	(이전 주소로 온 우편물을 다시 보낼) 새 주소[전송처]
Fragile	깨지기 쉬워 주의를 요하는
Free Port	자유항 싱가폴이나 홍콩과 같이 선박에 의해서 수입되는 화물에 세금이 부과되지 않는 항구
French Service	주방장이나 요리사가 고객 앞에서 직접 요리하여 제공하는 방식

Fried Eggs	OverEasy(Turn Over), Sunny Side Up
Front Office Cashier	고객의 계산, 귀중품 보관, 모든 계산, 환전업무 취급
Front Office Manager	우리나라에서 보통 객실과장이 이 업무를 맡으며, 현관 스텝들의 업무 지도 및 감독, 통솔한다
Full Course	격식과 순서에 의해 제공되는 정찬

G	
Gift Shop	토산품 판매소
Government Formalities	출입국 절차 (Customs, Immigration, Quarantine)
Grand Master Key	객실 전체를 열수 있는 열쇠
Green Channel	면세 검사대

H	
High Season	관광객이 많은 성수기. Peak Season, Tourist Much Season
Hospitality Desk	(단체용) 안내 카운터
Hospitality Room	총지배인, 현관지배인의 허락 하에 관광단체의 수하물을 임시로 보관한다든지 의상을 잠시 갈아입는 등의 특수한 경우에 무료로 사용하는 객실
Hotel Coupon	호텔이용권

I	
Immigration	이민, 입국심사
Inflight	기내의, 비행중의
International Date Line	국제 날짜 변경선

Itinerary	여행 일정표

J	
Jet Lag	신체의 시차 부적응 현상
Jet Stream	제트기류, 중위고도 상공을 일정하게 부는 바람

L	
Lavatory	화장실
Layover	직행 항공편이 없어서 가장 빠른 연결편을 탑승할 때까지 기다림
Limousine Bus	공항버스
Linen	테이블 클로스, 냅킨, 드랩스 등을 총칭하여 부르는 말
Local Time	현지시간(Zone Time)
Low Season	비수기

M	
Main Dining Room	주식당
Morning Call	호텔에 숙박한 고객이 다음날 아침, 시간을 정해서 전화로 깨워 주기를 부탁하는 것
Motel	Motorist'sHotel

N	
Night Shift	야근
No Arrivals	호텔에서 특별기간의 예약 때문에 예약을 받지 않는 것

O	
Occupancy Rate	호텔 객실 이용률. 항공기의 좌석 이용률
Occupancy Ratio	총판매 가능 객실 수 중에서 실제 판매된 객실 수에 대한 비율
Off Peak Rate	비수기 때의 호텔요금
Off Season	비수기
OnChange	객실 정돈 중이라는 표시로서 고객이 객실에서 퇴숙하고 난 뒤 아직 청소가 완료되지 않은 상태
On-season Fare	성수기의 운임이며 보통운임 객실료
One Way Fare	편도 운임
Open Ticket	예약은 했으나 구체적으로 날짜가 기재되어 있지 않은 항공권
Outbound	한국인의 외국여행(↔inbound 외국인의 한국여행)

P	
Package Tour	Tour Operator에 의해 숙식, 관광 등이 미리 짜여진 특별한 상품
Peak Season	성수기
Pension	유럽에서 발전된 전형적인 하숙식 여인숙으로 소규모의 객실접대도 극히 제한된 서비스만 제공하며 숙박비도 저렴하다

Q	
Quarantine	검역

R	
Reconfirm	예약을 재확인하다(Reconfirmation)
Room Rack	객실 상황을 포괄하는 것

Room Service	호텔 객실의 고객 요청으로 음료, 식사 등을 보내 주는 담당계 혹은 호텔의 객실에서 하는 식사. 객실에 투숙 중인 고객의 편의를 위해 식사, 음료 등을 객실에 운반하는 서비스를 행하거나 영업과 관계된 고객의 요청사항을 대행하는 호텔 식음부의 영업부서
Round Ticket	왕복티켓(↔One Way Ticket 편도티켓)

S	
Safety Box	안전금고
Scrambled Eggs	계란 2개 반과 우유 큰 스푼을 섞어 저은 후 미리 버터를 녹여 놓은 후라이 팬에 붓고 약한 불로 저어 만든 계란 요리
Shift	근무조, 근무시간
Single Room	한 명이 이용하는 객실
Sleep Out	외박 고객. 객실료를 지불했으나 등록한 객실에서 숙박하지 않고 외부에서 숙박한 고객
Suite Room	침실과 응접실이 연결된 VIP를 위한 객실

T	
Tariff	항공과 화물 운임에 관한 관련규정을 수록해 놓은 운임표
TaxFree	면세
Tour Conductor	여행안내자
Transportation	교통기관
Travel Agent	여행대리점
Travel Plant	여행시설, 관광시설
Traveller's Check	여행자 수표
Transit Passenger	통과여객, 경유손님

Travel Agency	여행사
Twin Room	두 개의 싱글 베드가 놓여진 객실

U	
Unchecked Baggage	기내 휴대 수화물
Utensil	주방 바에서 사용하는 기물의 총칭

V	
Vacancy	빈 객실. 풀 하우스가 아닌 상태로 판매 가능 객실이 아직 남아 있음을 의미
Vending Machine	간단한 식료나 음료 또는 담배 따위를 판매원의 도움 없이 판매하는 자동판매기
Ventilation	통풍
VIP	VeryImportant Person. 중요한 손님. 특별한 대접을 위해 정해지고 사전에 등록된 고객
VISA	사증

W ~	
Waiting List	이미 예약이 만원이 되어 있는 좌석 또는 호텔 객실의 취소를 기다리고 있는 사람의 명부
Wake-up Call	MorningCall
Yellow Card	예방접종 증명서
Youth Fare	학생할인
Youth Hostel	청소년을 위한 저렴한 숙박시설. 대중관광의 일환으로 발전한 청년여행과 직결되어 성장을 보여주고 있는 젊은이를 위한 숙소

부록 8. American Conversational Expressions

Absolutely not.	절대 아닙니다.
Act your age.	철 좀 들어라.
Action will be taken soon.	조치가 곧 취해질 겁니다.
Any comments?	의견 있나요?
Anytime will be fine.	언제든 좋아요.
Are we allowed to take pictures in here?	여기에서 사진을 찍어도 괜찮나요?
Are you decent?	들어가도 되니?
Are you two close?	둘이 사이가 좋나요?
As good as can be expected.	더 이상 바랄 수 없을 정도죠.
Be my guest.	(상대방의 부탁을 들어주며) 그러세요.
Because of you, I'm in a bad mood.	너 때문에 기분이 나빠.
Better late than not.	안하는 것보다 늦은 것이 더 낫다.
Bite your tongue!	말조심해.
Both sides refuse to fold.	양측이 팽팽히 맞서있다.
Business is business.	공과 사는 구별해야지.
Can I bring you anything?	내가 준비할 거 있니?
Can I tempt you?	한잔할래.
Can we get the bill?	계산서 좀 주실래요.

Can you be more specific?	좀 구체적으로 말해주실래요?
Can you come down a little on this?	깎아 주실래요?
Can you save my place in line?	자리 좀 지켜주실래요?
Catch you later.	이따 보자.
Cold is better.	차가울수록 좋아.
Could I speak with the manager, please?	당신 상사와 얘기할 수 있나요?
Could you pull up here?	여기서 세워주실래요?
Cut it out!	집어 치워!
Did you get all that?	다 적었나요?
Do I look like I am easy?	내가 만만하게 보이니?
Do we have everyone?	다 탔나요?
Do you have a first-aid kit?	구급상자 있으세요?
Do you have any recommendations?	추천하실 만한 것이 있나요?
Do you have anything cheaper?	더 싼 것은 없나요?
Do you live on or off campus?	학교 안에서 사나요, 아님 밖에서 사나요?
Do you take cream in your coffee?	커피크림 넣으세요?
Do you want to grab a bite?	뭐 좀 먹을까?
Don't be pushy.	강요하지 마.
Don't beat around the bush!	빙빙 돌리지 말고 핵심을 말해.
Don't beat the air.	헛수고하지 마.

Don't get technical.	어려운 말마라.
Don't go too far.	너무 오버 하지 마.
Don't hit my nerve.	내 성질 건들지 마.
Don't jump to conclusions.	섣불리 판단하지 마세요.
Don't keep me in suspense.	어서 이야기 해봐요.
Don't kill yourself over it.	그런 문제로 자신을 혹사시키지 마.
Don't make it any worse than it is.	일을 더 악화시키지 마라.
Don't open up too fast.	쉽게 마음을 주지 마.
Don't order me around.	이래라 저래라 명령하지 마.
Don't sit your hands.	빈둥거리지 마.
Don't take it personally.	너 들으라고 한 소리가 아니야.
Don't talk to me like that.	듣기 싫어요.
Don't try to drag me into this.	이 일에 끌어들이려 하지 마.
Drop by if you're in the neighborhood.	근처에 오면 들르세요.
Everybody has a skeleton in his closet.	털어서 먼지 안 나는 사람 없어.
Everybody turns in your assignments at the end of class.	수업후 과제를 제출해 주세요.
Everything seems like a waste of time.	모든 게 시간 낭비인 것 같아.
Everything will turn out fine.	모든 게 좋아질 거야.

Excuse my appearance.	이런 꼴로 맞게 되어 미안해요.
Fair's fair.	좋은 것이 좋은 것이다.
Get a hair cut?	머리 좀 깎아라.
Get a life!	정신 차려!
Get it off your chest.	속 시원히 털어놔 봐.
Give me another opportunity.	한번만 기회를 더 주세요.
Give me the bottom line.	요점만 말해.
Go out and get some air.	나가서 바람 좀 쐐.
Good point.	좋은 지적이야.
Got a minute?	시간 있니?
Hang on a second.	잠깐 기다려.
Have it your way.	좋을 대로 해.
Have we ever met before?	우리가 전에 만난 적 있나요?
Have you ever been on any medication?	약을 복용한 적이 있나요?
He cuts me in the street.	그는 나를 모르는 척 해.
He got canned.	그는 해고됐어.
He has poor social skills.	그는 사교성이 없어.
He is a baby face.	그는 동안이다.
He is at the top of the tree.	그가 일인자야.
He is eating dirt.	그가 모욕을 참고 있어.
He is short of generosity.	그는 도량이 부족해.

He is talking down to me.	그는 나를 무시하며 말해.
He is under fire.	그는 비난받고 있어.
He looks so dejected.	그는 너무 풀이 죽어 보여.
He puts his foot in his mouth.	그는 함부로 말해.
He rings his own bell.	그는 자화자찬 해.
He's a has-been.	그는 한물갔어.
He's direct in talking.	그는 직선적으로 말해.
He's got a heavy heart.	그는 무거운 심정이야.
He's got a one-track mind.	그는 융통성이 없다.
He's got no courage.	그는 용기가 없어.
He's on the ball.	그는 빈틈이 없어.
He's totally lost his cool.	그는 완전히 이성을 잃어버렸다.
He's very disturbed.	정신적으로 불안정해요.
Hold your horses.	진정하세요.
How can I get in touch with you?	어떻게 연락하지?
How could you treat me like this?	네가 나를 어떻게 이렇게 대할 수 있니?
How did you do that?	어떻게 하셨어요?
How long has you been?	이게 얼마만이에요?
How long will it take to develop the pictures?	사진 현상하는데 얼마나 걸리나요?
How many people are you expecting?	몇 명 정도 올 것 같나요?

How much did you put down?	계약금은 얼마 지불했죠?
How much is it all together?	전부해서 얼마죠?
How much longer will my order take?	주문한 것을 얼마나 더 기다려야죠?
How often do you work out?	운동은 얼마나 자주 하죠?
How was your day?	오늘 하루 어땠어요?
How's business going?	사업이 어떻게 되어갑니까?
I almost forgot your face.	네 얼굴 잊어버리겠다.
I am pressed for time.	나는 시간에 쫓기고 있어.
I apologize for the inconvenience.	불편하게 해 드려서 죄송해요.
I blacked out.	필름이 끊겼다.
I can't answer that at present.	현재는 대답할 수 없어요.
I can't answer that at present.	난 네가 나한테 이런 짓을 했다니 믿기가 어려워.
I can't eat another bite.	더 이상 못 먹어.
I can't handle the heat.	더운 것은 못 참어.
I can't make ends meet.	형편이 어려워.
I can't pinpoint it.	꼭 집어 말하기 어려워.
I can't put a face to the name.	이름과 얼굴을 매치시키지 못하겠어.
I couldn't sleep a wink.	한숨도 못 잤다.
I did a double check.	두 번 검사했어.
I did them myself.	제가 직접 했어요.

I didn't mean to do that.	결코 고의가 아니야.
I didn't quite hear you.	잘 듣지 못했어요.
I don't care to hear more.	더 듣고 싶지 않소.
I don't feel well about it.	나도 맘이 편하지 않아.
I don't need your sympathy.	네 동정은 필요하지 않아.
I don't see the end of this.	도대체 끝이 안 보이네.
I feel a big burden to do it.	그것을 하는 데 큰 부담을 느끼고 있다.
I feel heavy.	몸이 찌뿌듯하다.
I feel it in my bones.	장담해.
I feel like a new person.	날아갈 것 같은 기분이야.
I feel like I know you already.	당신을 이미 알고 있는 것 같아요.
I forgot where I last had it.	어디다 두었는지 몰라요.
I get really nervous in public.	대중 앞에서 초조해요.
I get the picture.	알았어요.
I get worn-out easily.	쉽게 피로해요.
I had mixed feelings about it.	기분이 교차했습니다
I have a company coming.	일행이 있어요.
I have a lot on my plate.	할일이 많아.
I have an early day tomorrow.	내일 일찍 일어나야해.
I have some laundry.	빨래가 있어요.
I have ten minutes to kill.	10분을 때워야해.

I have to slim down.	살을 빼야해.
I hope I didn't offend you.	기분을 상하게 하지 않았으면 해요.
I hope it's nothing serious.	심각한 게 아니길 바랍니다.
I just came one step ahead of you.	당신 보다 조금 먼저 왔어요.
I know how you feel about it.	당신 기분을 알아요.
I let you down.	너를 실망시켰어.
I moonlight.	나는 부업을 해.
I must know what it is.	난 그게 뭔지 알아야겠어.
I need a bit more time.	시간이 좀 더 필요해요
I need to get some shut-eye.	잠 좀 자야 돼.
I need to take your blood pressure.	혈압 좀 재야겠습니다.
I never forget a face	한번 보면 기억해.
I never said that!	그런 말 한적 없다.
I ran out of time and didn't get finished.	나는 시간에 쫓겨서 다 끝내지 못했어.
I really learned a lot in that class.	저는 그 수업에서 많은 것을 배웠습니다.
I think I've taken up too much of your time.	제가 시간을 너무 많이 뺏은 것 같아요.
I think there's a leak somewhere.	어딘가에서 새요.
I totally lost my composure.	난 완전히 침착성을 잃었어.

I want to express my appreciation.	감사의 말을 전하고 싶어요.
I want to put in for a raise.	급여인상을 신청하려고요.
I want you to take back what you just said.	방금 그 말 취소해.
I was at a loss what to say.	뭐라 해야 할지 몰랐어.
I was born and raised here.	전 이곳 토박이입니다.
I was born for this.	난 타고난 체질이야.
I was here before.	전에 왔었는데요.
I was humiliated.	창피했습니다.
I was tied up on the freeway.	교통체증에 묶여있어.
I was tongue tied.	말문이 막혔다.
I wasn't born yesterday.	난 애송이가 아냐.
I wish I could turn back the clock.	시간을 되돌릴 수만 있다면.
I work the night shift.	야간 근무입니다.
I'd like to make an appointment.	예약하려고요.
I'll be busy all weekend.	주말 내내 바쁠 거야.
I'll be done soon.	곧 다해요.
I'll go first.	제가 먼저 하죠.
I'll hang up and call again.	끊고 다시 걸죠.
I'll keep my eyes open for you	눈여겨 볼 거야.
I'll keep you in my prayers.	항상 기도해 드릴게요.

I'll pay for this.	제가 지불할게요.
I'll take care of my business.	내 일은 내가 할 거야.
I'm a moderate drinker.	나는 술을 적당히 마십니다.
I'm all booked up today.	나 오늘 바빠.
I'm all in.	지쳤어.
I'm all thumbs today.	오늘은 실수투성이다.
I'm behind in my work.	일이 밀렸어.
I'm done for the day.	일과를 다 마쳤어요.
I'm expecting company.	올 사람이 있어요.
I'm far too outspoken.	내가 지나치게 언성을 높였어.
I'm finished.	드디어 해냈어.
I'm going back to bed.	좀 누워야겠어.
I'm heading in the same direction.	같은 방향입니다.
I'm just a little under the weather.	몸이 안 좋아요.
I'm just about to call you.	막 전화하려고 했어.
I'm just browsing.	그냥 둘러보고 있어요.
I'm not getting in the middle of this.	이 일에 끼고 싶지 않아.
I'm on cloud nine.	매우 기뻐.
I'm positive.	정말이야.
I'm returning a call.	답신 전화입니다
I'm speechless.	말문이 막힌다.

I'm sure you would have done the same for me.	당신도 저한테 그렇게 해 줬을 거예요.
I'm under a lot of pressure.	많이 시달리고 있어요.
I'm walking on air.	매우 기쁘다.
I'm with him.	그와 동행이다.
I've seen everything.	별일 다 보는군.
Is it too late to get a refund?	환불받으려고 하는데 늦었나요?
Is there a cure?	치료법이 있나요?
Is this all you have?	이게 전부 인가요?
Is this seat taken?	자리 있나요?
It fits you well.	잘 어울려요.(의류에 관하여)
It has a lovely view.	경치 참 좋아요.
It hurts my conscience.	양심에 걸려요.
It is once in a lifetime chance.	평생 있을까 말까한 기회야.
It just melts in your mouth.	입에서 살살 녹는다.
It just slipped out.	그건 무심코 한 말이다.
It looks fake.	가짜 같아요.
It serves him right.	자업자득이지.
It takes two to tango.	손바닥도 마주 쳐야 소리가 나.
It was all my fault.	그건 모두 제 잘못이에요.
It was wrong from the beginning.	처음부터 잘못됐다.
It won't hurt to try.	해봐서 해될 것 없어

It's a long short.	가능성이 희박해.
It's a pretty short notice.	너무 갑작스런 부탁이지.
It's a real eyesore.	정말 꼴불견이야.
It's all kinds of technical terms.	내용이 너무 전문적이야.
It's around the corner.	머지않았어.
It's dead ahead.	막다른 길이야.
It's happened before.	전에도 있었던 일이잖아.
It's just one of those things.	어쩔 수 없는 일이잖아.
It's my turn to pay.	내가 살 차례야
It's not your mistake.	당신 잘못이 아니에요.
It's now or never!	지금 아니면 안 돼.
It's too late for that.	너무 늦었어요.
It's up to you.	너 하기에 달렸어.
Just be yourself.	침착하세요.
Just do it.	한 번 해봐요.
Just in case.	만약을 대비해서.
Just chicken feed.	쥐꼬리만큼.
Just leave her alone.	그녀를 그냥 내버려둬.
Just let me know when you're finished.	끝나면 내게 얘기해 줘요.
Just promise one thing.	하나만 약속해줘.
Keep away from me!	내게서 물러서요!

Keep it to yourself!	너만 알고 있어!
Keep your complaint to yourself.	불평 그만 좀 해라.
Knock it off!	그만둬!
Let me clarify that for you.	제가 명확히 설명하죠.
Let me get that for you.	제가 가져다 드릴게요.
Let me sleep on it.	곰곰이 생각해 볼게요.
Let's face facts.	사실을 직시해라.
Let's give him a big hand.	그에게 큰 박수를 보내죠.
Let's go by the book.	원칙 대로해.
Let's go for it.	해보자.
Let's let sleeping dogs lie.	긁어 부스럼 만들지 말자.
Let's make it a rush.	서두르자.
Let's stop playing word games.	말장난 그만 하자.
Let's pass the hat.	돈을 걷자.
Make sense anyway.	그럴 듯해요.
May I ask the nature of your business?	용건이 뭐죠?
Maybe more than that.	그이상일지도 모르지.
Mistakes happen.	실수란 생기게 마련이야.
My chest feels heavy.	숨쉬기가 힘들어요.
My position is very uncomfortable.	내 입장이 난처해.
My vision is blurry.	시야가 흐려요.

No big deal!	별거 아냐!
No two ways about it.	두말하면 잔소리.
No way!	안 돼.
Not much, same old.	그냥 그렇지.
Not on your life.	말도 안 되는 소리.
Not this time.	지금은 좀 곤란해요.
Now you're talking.	이제야 말이 통하는 구나.
Over my dead body.	내 눈에 흙이 들어갈 때까진 안 돼.
Period!	할 말 다했어!
Picture to yourself.	상상해보렴.
Please be careful when you exit.	나가실 때 조심하세요.
Please be more careful in the future!	다음엔 좀 더 신중해라!
Please drop me off here.	여기서 내려주세요.
Please put in a word for me.	잘 좀 얘기해 주세요.
Pop quiz!	깜짝 시험이야.
Pull over at the next area.	다음 휴게소에서 차를 세워.
Pull your own weight.	힘내렴.
Put a lid on it.	상관하지 마.
Ridiculous.	말도 안 되는군요.
Same to you.	너하고 같아.
Say your piece.	소신 것 말해.

Settle down back there.	거기서 잠잠히 있어라.
She blew her top.	그녀는 머리끝까지 화가 났어.
She has a big mouth.	그녀는 입이 싸다.
She is all legs.	그녀는 키가 커.
She is two-faced.	그녀는 이중인격자야.
She's a good talker.	그녀는 말이 청산유수다.
She's very moody.	그녀는 변덕이 심해.
Since when?	언제부터?
So what?	그래서 어쨌다고?
Sometimes your criticism is too much.	가끔 네 비판이 지나쳐.
Step aside!	비켜!
Step on it, please.	빨리 가주세요.
Swallow your pride.	자존심은 버려
Take a free sample.	무료상품을 가져가세요.
Take your pick.	고르세요.
Tell me what happened.	무슨 일이 있었는지 말해봐.
That explains a lot.	그건 많은 의미가 있어.
That was my best time.	그때가 가장 행복했어요.
That's a private matter.	그건 비밀이지.
That's a rip off.	바가지 쓰셨군요.
That's an icing on the cake.	금상첨화다.

That's really super!	엄청나네요.
That's the deal!	그러자.
That's the name of the game.	그것이 핵심이야.
The price is right.	가격이 적당하다.
The sooner we start, the easier it will be.	빨리 시작할수록 일이 쉬어질 거야.
The test will be timed.	시험은 시간제한이 있을 겁니다.
There is a fly in the ointment.	옥에 티다.
There might be another way.	다른 방법이 있을 거야.
There's not such things as a free lunch!	세상에 공짜가 없다.
They are for the birds.	시시해.
Think nothing of it.	별거 아닙니다.
This doesn't involve you.	넌 이일에 상관없어.
This is a little something for you	조그만 선물입니다.
This problem runs in my family.	가족 내력입니다.
Time will tell.	시간이 약이야.
Time's up.	시간이 다 됐습니다.
Use your imagination.	머리 좀 써라.
Watch your language!	말조심해.
We have a lot in common.	우리는 통하는 게 많아.
We have to cut costs.	비용을 줄여야 합니다.
We're short of time.	시간이 없어요.

What do you do when you're free?	시간 날 때 뭐하죠?
What's going on?	어떻게 된 거죠?
What's on your mind?	뭐 신경 쓰는 거라도 있니?
Who cares about it?	까짓 거 뭐.
Who's in charge?	책임자가 누구죠?
You don't have to answer right away.	바로 대답할 필요 없어.
You hit the nail on the head.	정곡을 찔렀어.
You name it.	말만하세요.
You say something.	뭐라고 말 좀 해보세요.
You will pay for this.	네가 한 말에 대가를 치룰 거야.
You've come a long way.	대단한 발전을 하셨군요.
You've got that backwards.	정 반대로 알고 있구나.
Your guess is as good as mine.	나도 모르지.

부록 9. ***Useful Expressions***

- ❏ seasonal variation 계절적 변수
- ❏ need to be watered 물을 줘야 한다
- ❏ prior to the current situation
  현재 상황에 앞서
- ❏ ahead of time 예정보다 빨리
- ❏ be related to each other 서로관련 되어 있다.
- ❏ on very short notice 매우 촉박한 통지를 받고
- ❏ for a higher price 좀 더 높은 가격에
- ❏ at regular intervals 일정한 간격으로
- ❏ on the waiting list 대기자 명단에
- ❏ out of stock 재고가 떨어진

- ❑ come close to the estimated amount
  그 추정치에 가까워지다.
- ❑ restore its reputation 그것의 명성을 되찾다.
- ❑ park in the reserved parking area
  지정한 주차 공간에 주차하다.
- ❑ be responsive to the needs
  요구에 응대하다.
- ❑ safety precautions 안전 예방 조치
- ❑ a chance of rain 비 올 가능성
- ❑ exposure to sunlight 햇빛에 노출
- ❑ on a regular basis 규칙적으로
- ❑ job opening 일자리
- ❑ a moderate decline 완만한 하강

❑ hiring freezes 고용동결

❑ the written consent of both parties
쌍방 동의서

❑ marginal interest in work
일에 대한 최소한 관심

❑ expiration date 만기일

❑ cautiously optimistic about future
미래를 조심스럽게 낙관하는

❑ put in for a transfer to go to the branch office 지사로 전근을 요청하다.

❑ direct participants to a dining room
참석자들에게 식당으로 가는 길을 알려주다

❑ perform critical tasks 중대한 일을 수행하다

❑ acquire professional experience
전문적인 경험을 얻다.

- ❑ increase our market share
  시장 점유율을 증가시키다.
- ❑ affect your profit 수익에 영향을 주다.
- ❑ maintain our good reputation
  좋은 평판을 유지하다.
- ❑ organize a workshop 워크샵을 준비하다.
- ❑ come into effect next year
  내년에 효력을 나타내다.
- ❑ a recent trend in fashion 최근 유행 경향
- ❑ the various factors 다양한 요인
- ❑ the possibility of an accident 사고 가능성
- ❑ ask for improvements to be made
  개선이 이루어질 것을 요청하다.
- ❑ one's daily transaction sheets 거래일지

- [ ] with no hesitation 아무런 주저 없이
- [ ] a shortage of parking on campus
  캠퍼스 내 주차 공간 부족
- [ ] provide practical experience
  실제 경험을 제공하다.
- [ ] damaged vehicles 손상된 차량
- [ ] a definite date 확정된 날짜
- [ ] strictly deal with labor disputes
  노동 쟁의를 엄격히 다루다.
- [ ] refrain from using cellular phones
  휴대폰 사용을 자제하다.
- [ ] forsee the problem 문제를 예견하다.
- [ ] minimize nutrient loss
  영양의 손실을 최소화하다.

- ❑ address the problem 그 문제에 대처하다.
- ❑ surpass all records 모든 기록을 능가하다.
- ❑ the cancellation of a reservation 예약취소
- ❑ after consideration 생각을 해본 후에
- ❑ the addition of new bus lines
  새로운 버스 노선 추가
- ❑ vehicle inspection 차량검사
- ❑ be mature for one's age 나이에 비해 성숙하다.
- ❑ habitual criminals 상습범
- ❑ set realistic goals 현실적인 목표를 정하다.
- ❑ pursue the plan aggressively
  계획을 적극적으로 추구하다.
- ❑ return it promptly 즉각 되돌려 보내다.

- [ ] inflate your life jacket
  구명조끼에 바람을 넣으세요.
- [ ] revise the contract 계약서를 수정하다.
- [ ] verify the price 금액을 확인하다.
- [ ] additional comments 부가 설명
- [ ] a lavish compensation package
  후한 보상 정책
- [ ] affordable for the average customer
  보통의 소비자들이 구입할 수 있는
- [ ] a deliberate attempt 고의적인 시도
- [ ] impaired vision 손상된 시력
- [ ] replacement parts 교체 부품
- [ ] world-class service 세계적인 수준의 서비스

- ❑ adjust automatically 자동적으로 조절하다.
- ❑ pressure from the competitors
  경쟁 상대들로부터의 압력
- ❑ a sophisticated scanner 정밀한 스캐너
- ❑ use recycled materials 재활용품을 사용하다.
- ❑ recover part of the losses
  손실의 일부를 회복하다.
- ❑ lower rates 요금을 내리다.
- ❑ miss a deadline 마감 시간을 놓치다.
- ❑ refuse to cooperate 협조하는 것을 거부하다.
- ❑ at no extra cost 추가비용 없이
- ❑ on a strike 파업중
- ❑ establish regulation 규정을 세우다.

- ❑ the final date for submission 최종 제출 일자
- ❑ apply for sick leave 병가를 신청하다.
- ❑ the performance evaluation files
  직무 평가 파일
- ❑ a letter of authorization 위임장
- ❑ the ability to interact 상호 작용할 수 있는 능력
- ❑ get through the preliminary interviews
  예상면접을 통과하다
- ❑ narrow down 범위를 좁혀나가다
- ❑ in observance of the national holiday
  국경일을 준수하여
- ❑ every hour on the hour 매시 정각에
- ❑ in the strongest possible terms
  가장 강력한 어조로

- ❑ remain to be seen 지켜보다
- ❑ reduce substantially 상당히 감소하다
- ❑ be temporarily out of stock
  일시적으로 매진되다
- ❑ can realistically expect
  실질적으로 기대할 수 있다.
- ❑ listen objectively 객관적으로 듣다
- ❑ rely heavily on 지나치게 의존하다
- ❑ under consideration 고려중
- ❑ be almost finished 거의 마무리되다
- ❑ must react calmy 신중히 대처하다
- ❑ be clustered around 주위에 몰려있다
- ❑ bold and original 대담하고 독창적인

- ❑ be restored to their original design
  원래 디자인 형태로 복원되다
- ❑ existing equipment 실재하는 장치
- ❑ updated manual 업데이트된 매뉴얼
- ❑ unexpected outcome 예기치 못한 결과
- ❑ cautiously optimistic 신중하게 낙관적인
- ❑ in times of prosperity 번영의 시기
- ❑ expiration dates 만기일
- ❑ dramatic scenery 아름다운 경치
- ❑ in a timely manner 시기적절한 방법으로
- ❑ discuss one's concerns about
  관심사를 논의하다
- ❑ long-term stability 장기적인 안전성

- ❑ the right to revise 수정할 권리
- ❑ for proper process 적절한 작업의 수행을 위해
- ❑ profound influence 상당한 영향력
- ❑ a pay increase 봉급인상
- ❑ retain freshness 신선함을 유지하다
- ❑ media coverage 언론보도 범위
- ❑ personal belongings 개인 소지품

부록 10. *Everyday Words*

Cleaning Supplies

feather duster

recycling bin

rubber gloves

stepladder

squeegee

dustpan

trash bags

vacuum cleaner

wet mop

dust mop

dish towel

sponge

cleanser

Getting sick

ache

ailment

allergy

backache

cough

dizzy

earache

fever

flu

headache

indigestion

nauseous

pain

sneeze

sore

sore throat

stiff neck

stomachache

toothache

Library

title

subject

stacks

library card

encyclopedia

due

check out

cart

author

Camping

wild animal

trailer

tent

sleeping bag

lantern

set up camp

backpack

campfire

At the Beach

waves

sunbathe

sunburn

surf

swim

sail

sailboat

shovel

bury

drown

lifeguard

beach blanket

Taking a trip

passport

luggage/baggage

sightseeing

suitcase

travel brochure

airplane ticket

tour

camera

At the Park

swings

water fountain

see saw

slide

picnic table

feed the birds

have a picnic

jungle gym

Movies

usher

ticket

sell

lobby

actor

actress

audience

collect

screen

Watching TV

variety show

soap opera

game show

drama

comedy

channel

comedian

Going out

theater

religious service

museum

guest

dressed up

amusement park

concert

club

sculpture

Leisure time

play with a pet

sing a song

go to the movies

go to a party

play the guitar

take photographs

travel

The Dentist

braces

cavity

cleaning

extraction

filling

Staying healthy

blood pressure

checkup

height

measure

weigh

weight

Safety at work

assembly line

co-worker

safety- violation

supervisor

mask

Jobs

barber

chef

mechanic

teacher aid

fisherman

farm worker

engineer

factory worker

mail carrier

manicurist

construction worker

Home Repairs

scissors

screw

needle

spool of thread

board

flashlight

locksmith

fuse box

gas meter

repair person

roofer

Everyday Work

wash the window

rake the leaves

dry the dishes

mop the floor

make the bed

put away the toys

dust the furniture

sweep the floor

feed the dog

hammer nail

do housework

cook a meal

change the bulb

vacuum the carpet

Gas Station

gas pump

inspection

repairs

tire

self-service

oil

lift

full service

Parts of a Car

windshield

turn signal

headlight

hood

bumper

gas tank

air conditioner

muffler

air bag

speedometer

license plate

heater

tape deck

globe compartment

front seat

seat belt

back seat

steering wheel

emergency brake

car key

accelerator

wheel

fuel gage

fender

clutch

gas cap

Traffic Signs

stop

school crossing

dead end

speed limit

one way

yield

Do not enter

school

steep hill

Cars

subcompact

compact

sports car

convertible

camper

tow truck

dup truck

trailer

Preposition of Moving

under the bridge
into the taxi
onto the highway
off the highway
around the corner
up the stairs
down the stairs

Transportation

bus stop
bus driver
fare
subway
train
taxi/cab
taxi stand
ferry
transfer
track
subway station
get on
get off
exact change
exit
passenger
wait a line

The Bank

save
savings account
money order
deposit slip
credit card
cash
cash a check
account

The Post Office

first class
insurance
letter
mail bag
mail box
postage
scale
stamp
postal clerk
third class

Emergency : police

witness
thief

steal
police report
owner
lost
arrest
break in
handcuffs
crime

Telephone

busy signal
cordless
wrong number
message
receiver
hold
long distance
hang up
answering machine

Neighborhood

building
convenient store
crosswalk
newstand
pizza shop
traffic sign
trash can
parking meter
laundromat

An Office

desk calendar
desk pad
file holder
supply cabinet
envelope
fax machine
appointment book
stapler
stapler
organizer
notepad
post-it notes
packing tape
glue
paper clip
rubber band
binder
greeting card
ruler

typing paper

Jewelry Store

wedding ring
ruby
necklace
emerald
diamond
chain
bracelet

Pharmacy

film
medicine
sunscreen
skin lotion
nail polish
tissues
vitamins
hair spray
diapers
pharmacist
mouthwash
makeup

Department Store

appliance
domestics
gift wrap
escalator
elevator
cosmetics
jewelry counter

Job Skills

sell cars
type
sew clothes
take care of
drive a truck
work on a computer

Fast Food

hamburger
soda
iced tea
hot dot
pizza
milk shake
counter
muffin
salad bar
straw

sugar
relish
nachos

The Market

bottle return
shopping cart
baked goods
dairy section
pet food
frozen foods
beverages
cash register
checker
soup
beans
rice
cookies
cake
eggs
butter
cheese
potato chips
gum
flour
apple juice
bottled water
plastic wrap
aluminumfoil

Chidren's Bedroom

bunk bed
mobile
dollhouse
ball
cradle
puzzle
toy chest
picture book
coloring book
smoke detector
blocks
teddy bear

A Bathroom

hamper
rubber mat
drain
faucet
towel rack

showerhead
toilet paper
mirror
toothbrush
sink
soap
wastebasket
bath mat
tile

A Kitchen

counter
drawer
electric mixer
broiler
burner
teakettle
microwaven oven
refrigerator
shelf
freezer
blender
toaster
garbage disposal

A House

fence
mailbox
driveway
garage
front door
steps
door bell
chimney
shutter
garage door
gutter

Apartments

roof garden
fire escape
parking space
intercom
peephole
door chain

A Graduation

buffet
guest
banner
hug
make a toast

dance

Feelings

thirsty

sleepy

comfortable

disgusted

calm

nervous

lonely

embarrassed

homesick

upset

surprised

tired

Daily Routines

wake up

take a shower

get dressed

go to work

leave work

cook dinner

read the paper

exercise

go to bed

go to sleep

The Body

ankle

arm

back

buttocks

calf

cheek

chest

chin

ear

elbow

exercise

face

finger

fingernail

forehead

hand

head

heel

hip

jaw

knee

leg

lip

mouth

neck

nose

shin

shoulder

sweat

thigh

thumb

toe

toenail

tooth

waist

work out

wrist

저자소개

문영수(文榮秀)

전북대학교 인문대 영어영문학과 졸업
고려대학교 대학원 영어영문학과 졸업(문학석사)
전북대학교 대학원 영어영문학과 졸업(문학박사)
광신대학교 신학대학원 졸업(목회학 석사)
총회신학원 수료
전북대학교 인문대 강사 역임
University of Wisconsin-Madison visiting professor(1993)
현) 호원대학교 관광대학 호텔관광학부 교수
현) 무디교회 담임목사

〈주요 저서〉
누워서 보는 영어(백산출판사, 2005) / 크게 웃고 가는 리딩스킬(백산출판사, 2005), Grammar Free Zone(백산출판사, 2010) 外 다수

〈주요 논문〉
우울증의 목회 상담적 치유 연구(2009) /
시대를 향한 한 시인의 노력: 브라우닝의 낙관주의 연구(2008) 外 다수

천재윤(하진)

현재 어학원과 대학에서 후학을 양성 중인 저자는 지금까지 17년 동안 대한민국 영어교육을 위해 노력해 왔다. 특히 영어학습자들의 지적 요구에 부응하기 위해 School Grammar에서 다루지 못하는 영역에 대해 활발히 연구 중이다.

Major/Sociolinguistics
University of Hawaii N.I.C.E Course (full scholarship)
Chonbuk National University Graduate School (full scholarship)

전) Bank of America
현) Win Language Academy Representative
현) Chonbuk National Univ. / Howon Univ. Visiting Prof.
현) The Sociolinguistic Society of Korea, The Linguistic Association of Korea member

〈주요 저서〉
누워서 보는 영어(백산출판사, 2005) / 크게 웃고 가는 리딩스킬(백산출판사, 2005) / 술술 내려 읽는 미국영어(백산출판사, 2006), Grammar Free Zone(백산출판사, 2010) 外 다수

〈주요 논문〉
A Sociolinguistic Study of Korean-English Code-Mixing in Korean Popular Songs 外

Survival Tourism English

2011년 2월 10일 초판 1쇄 인쇄
2011년 2월 15일 초판 1쇄 발행

저 자 문영수·천재윤
발행인 (寅製) 진 욱 상

발행처 백산출판사
서울시 성북구 정릉3동 653-40
등록 : 1974. 1. 9. 제 1-72호
전화 : 914-1621, 917-6240
FAX : 912-4438
http://www.ibaeksan.kr
editbsp@naver.com

값 12,000원
ISBN 978-89-6183-430-8